JULIA ARIAS

WHEN TO WALK AWAY. HOW TO LEAVE BEHIND THE PAST

HEALING FROM TOXIC RELATIONSHIPS

© Copyright 2024 - Julia Arias - All rights reserved.

The purpose of this document is to provide accurate and reliable information on the topic and issue at hand. The book is sold with the understanding that the publisher is not obligated to provide accounting, legally permitted, or otherwise qualified services. If legal or professional advice is required, a well-versed professional should be consulted.

- From a Declaration of Principles that was unanimously accepted and approved by an American Bar Association Committee and a Committee of Publishers and Associations.

Any part of this document, whether in electronic or printed format, may not be reproduced, duplicated, or transmitted in any way. The recording of this publication is strictly prohibited, and storage of this document is only permitted with the publisher's written permission. All intellectual property rights are reserved.

The information provided herein is stated to be true and consistent in that any liability arising from the use or abuse of any policies, processes, or directions contained herein, whether due to inattention or otherwise, is solely and completely the responsibility of the recipient reader. Under no circumstances will the publisher be held liable for any reparation, damages, or monetary loss incurred as a result of the information contained herein, whether directly or indirectly.

All copyrights not held by the publisher belong to the authors.

The information provided here is solely for educational purposes and is therefore universal. The information is presented without any type of contract or guarantee assurance.

The trademarks are used without the trademark owner's permission or backing, and the trademark is published without the trademark owner's permission or backing. All trademarks and brands mentioned in this book are the property of their respective owners and are not affiliated with this document.

TABLE OF CONTENTS

INTRODUCTION	7
CHAPTER 1: RECOGNIZING RELATIONSHIP RED FLAGS	9
Red Flags to Look Out For	9
CHAPTER 2: FIND A MIDDLE GROUND IN THE RELATIONSHIP	16
CHAPTER 3: REDUCE RELATIONSHIP CONFLICTS	21
CHAPTER 4: NARCISSISTIC CONTROL TACTICS	27
CHAPTER 5: DETERMINING TOXICITY IN A RELATIONSHIP	33
Type of Toxic Partners	34
Toxic Relationship and Its Signs	35
CHAPTER 6: NARCISSISTIC ABUSE	39
CHAPTER 7: STARTING THE HEALING PROCESS	46
How to Start the Healing Process	46
Tips on How to Get Over a Toxic Relationship	48
CHAPTER 8: IMPORTANCE OF NO CONTACT	52
No Contact: What It Is and What It Isn't	52
CHAPTER 9: HOW TO HEAL THE BRAIN FROM RELATIONSHIP TRAUMA	58
How Emotional Trauma Changes the Brain	59
Healing the Brain After Relationship trauma	60
CHAPTER 10: HOW TO STOP A NARCISSISTIC ABUSE CYCLE	64
What is The Narcissistic Cycle of Abuse	64
How to Stop the Cycle of Abuse	66
CHAPTER 11: SET BOUNDARIES WITH TOXIC PEOPLE	71
CHAPTER 12: REBUILD SELF-ESTEEM AFTER GETTING OUT OF A TOXIC RELATIONSHIP	78
CHAPTER 13: TOXIC RELATIONSHIPS AND ITS FORMS	84
CHAPTER 14: MOVING ON AFTER A TOXIC RELATIONSHIP	90

CHAPTER 15: REALITY OF HEALING	96
The Painful Truth of Overcoming a Toxic Relationship	97
CHAPTER 16: HEALING FROM EMOTIONAL TRAUMA	101
What Is Emotional Trauma?	102
How to Heal From Emotional Trauma	103
CHAPTER 17: HOW TO CREATE HEALTHY RELATIONSHIPS	108
CHAPTER 18: TIPS TO KEEP IN MIND	113
CONCLUSION	118

INTRODUCTION

Congratulations on purchasing Healing From Toxic Relationships: When to Walk Away. How to Leave Behind the Past, and thank you for doing so.

Human beings always try to be physically and emotionally close to each other. There is no doubt that life can feel better when shared. But there is no other human activity that tends to be more filled with hardships and hurdles than our interactions with other people. Relationships take work. Toxic relationships require more work. No one is perfect in this world: your close friends, parents, and even your partner. However, there are certain relationships that tend to be more challenging.
Such relationships require more effort.

Some people in relationships are most likely to face bigger problems or more arguments. Then come all those connections that are poisonous by nature. Such interactions tend to take such a shape that they might end up damaging our overall well-being.

Relationships of this kind are not doomed inherently. But they require extensive effort and work if you want to change them into anything healthy.
A toxic relationship is a connection in which the behaviors or actions of the toxic partner are not destructive in their eyes. We will discuss toxic relationships in detail and how someone can get rid of one.

There are plenty of books on this subject on the market; thanks again for
choosing this one! Every effort was made to ensure it is full of as much useful
information as possible; please enjoy!

CHAPTER 1
RECOGNIZING RELATIONSHIP RED FLAGS

It is true for all of us – a new relationship with a person we like can make us feel like walking on cloud nine. However, a seemingly match made in heaven is powerful enough to make you go blind to negative behaviors or actions. It might include personality disorders like narcissistic personality disorder, antisocial personality disorder, borderline personality disorder, and so on. There might be red flags in a relationship – some signs that can determine something is amiss. Red flags are signs that you can easily see in the new love interest of your friend but are invisible to you in your relationship. Red flags are powerful enough to make a romantic relationship become a painful and ugly connection when ignored.

Red Flags to Look Out For

What are relationship red flags? Here are some red flags that can help you in your relationship.

PHYSICAL ABUSE

Physical abuse of any kind should always be taken seriously. In case you tend to feel scared by how a person is, or if they behave in certain physically threatening or abusive ways, that should be handled as it is required to be. It would be better for you to give a complete no to such things right from the beginning. No matter what the context is, physical abuse should never be entertained.

UNTREATED MENTAL HEALTH PROBLEMS

Another red flag in any relationship is an untreated mental health problem. It does not indicate that people with mental health issues cannot have normal or healthy relationships.

Of course, they can. But when conditions are left as it is, it might make a relationship quite challenging. It is something that is required to be stabilized.

MASTER MANIPULATOR

In case you feel an obligation, guilt, or fear, the chances are high that you are being manipulated. A manipulator will opt for various ways to manipulate you into providing them with what they want. In the end, you will be left disoriented and powerless. An easy way of describing manipulation is an attempt to get someone else to act in a specific way or make them feel in a particular way. All of us are guilty of manipulation at one point or the other. Generally, it is harmless such as attempting to get your partner to select a restaurant or making a decision about where to go for vacation. However, a master manipulator is someone who needs to be avoided at all costs. The most effective tool they use is fear. They might use violence or threaten you to attain their goals.

Another common tool manipulators use is the silent treatment. In case you do not do all they want, they will simply stop conversing with you. In fact, they might act in a way that you do not exist.

RUSHING A NEW RELATIONSHIP

Also known as love bombing, it is a red flag that is not about a partner who says "I love you" quickly or who wants to stay together after a few dates. Love bombing turns out to be worrying when a person tries their best to manipulate another person into a dependency or situation. For instance, if your partner says, "I cannot live without you," it can be regarded as a sign of concern. A fast-moving relationship can be okay as long as it feels correct. Try to check in with your body. In case you feel anxious regarding your partner moving too quickly, it could be a sign to apply brakes and determine where your feeling stems from.

DESCRIBES ALL EXES AS "CRAZY"

There are relationships that end on a bad note, and it can make you hate your ex even after a few years. However, if your partner refers to all their exes as crazy all the time, it could be an indication that they are the problem here. When your partner isn't aware of some of the ways in which they were also a part of their past breakups, it could be a sign of caution. If you also stop dating them, the chances are high that you will end up in the group of "crazy exes," too.

THEIR ANGER MAKES YOU FEEL UNSAFE

Anger is a natural emotion. When you are in a relationship, there will be times when you would feel like burying your face in the pillow and screaming. With that said, in case your partner gets so angry that they end up breaking household items or punching a wall, they might have the potential to escalate all such behaviors in the future. As anger management issues might escalate to abuse, they could be surefire signs of ending the relationship as soon as possible.

CANNOT LISTEN TO YOU

Here, we are not discussing your partner forgetting to get the groceries or the need to remind them of the name of your aunt's husband. It refers to all those significant aspects of yourself that you like to share with your partner, such as your traditions, interests, people you like, and so on. A useful question that you can ask yourself is, "How does he/she care for my interests and all those things that are important to me?" Communication can be regarded as the key here. In case you feel that you are not being heard or seen, you can ask your partner, "Can you understand how important this is for me?"
If this question can result in improvement, that is great. But if it shows no sign of improvement, keep in mind that an individual who is unwilling to grow is not worth your time.

BEING TOO CLINGY

In case a person you are dating is excessively clingy, that can be regarded as another red flag. But what is "too clingy?" A person who tries to be by your side all the time is too clingy. The life of such an individual starts and ends with you. They have got nothing in life outside of their relationship with you. It could feel like they are being glued at the hip. Whenever you want to spend some on your own, they are most likely to accuse you of not loving them. No matter what is the case, personal time is necessary. In case your partner desires to do everything with you, and you find them having no life outside of you, that is a red flag you need to watch out for.

VAGUE/KEEP SECRETS

In case the person you date is secretive and vague, you need to be aware. If they refuse to talk about their past, tell you anything about their family, or what they do for work, there has to be something happening behind the curtains. There are certain ways in which you can determine if your partner is keeping secrets from you.

- They do not leave their phone in your hands. They receive calls in another room, take them everywhere, and never share the passcode.

- They suddenly behave like the nicest person in the world. Although this might not seem that bad, it could be in case it deviates from their usual behavior.

- They do not share where they have been or where they are going.

- They tend to overreact as you confront them. They tend to make you feel mad for asking about it.

GASLIGHTS YOU

If your partner tends to gaslight you, you might be dealing with a huge problem. Narcissists are experts at this. But what is gaslighting? It can be regarded as a kind of manipulation.
A gaslighter will make you doubt yourself, besides making you feel as if you are crazy. It might get done in various ways.
For instance, they might minimize your feelings or make you feel they are of no importance. Also, they are most likely to

accuse you of overreacting. Another common technique of gaslighting is to counter anything you say. They might make up new details, question your memory, or even deny that anything happened. Slowly, you might start to lose faith in yourself and also question everything that you remember. Trying to live with such a person is more like living in a mental hell. Try to get away as fast as you can.

ISOLATES YOU FROM FRIENDS AND FAMILY

A person who tries their best or demands to keep you from your friends and family could be a huge concern. It might start with small steps. For instance, your partner might say, "Can you please stay home tonight? I want you near me." You might feel flattered at the start; however, slowly, this would change into a pattern. When your partner wants to keep you only for themselves, it could be an indication of a domestic situation starting. They might start to alienate you from those who are close to you. With time, you will feel that you have got no one in your life but him/her. That is how your toxic partner wants it. It is a definite red flag that you need to pay attention to in a relationship. No matter what is the case, any kind of isolation is not flattering; it is dangerous.

CRITICIZE ALL THE TIME

All of us can be critical of the behaviors and ideas of others sometimes. However, when the same thing is done with the intention of hurting or belittling someone, and that is too frequent, it is not healthy. Critical individuals can make you feel unworthy or inadequate. They will tend to disrespect you all the time, along with your words, behaviors, and thoughts. In fact, they might tend to humiliate you when with others.

However, there might be people who are concerned about how others see them. So, they will try to criticize you in private to seem caring and kind. Anytime when a person makes you feel that you are not intelligent enough, good enough, or that your ideas are worthless, the warning bells need to go off.

BEING SELF-CENTERED

Every human being can be self-centered from time to time. It is often regarded as an important aspect of self-preservation. Self-centered people keep thinking of themselves all the time. In fact, they might tend to discount or ignore the feelings of other people. They will demand you to meet their requirements, with no sort of reciprocation on their part.

Such people might make you responsible for their moods and happiness. In simple terms, whenever care, generosity, and consideration do not flow in both ways; it is a red flag.

CHAPTER 2
FIND A MIDDLE GROUND IN THE RELATIONSHIP

As you argue with your partner about something, it might feel impossible at times to reach a common ground. However, compromising in a relationship can be easier when you use certain key tips. Ensuring being calm and listening carefully can go a long way in attaining a proper solution that can work for you and your partner. It is true that compromise is an important component of a lasting relationship. But there is no need to be willing to abandon every stance. It is necessary to be aware of when you can work in the direction of finding common ground and when to be firm with your views.

There are certain boundaries that should never be compromised. A person should not compromise themselves or their boundaries with a partner. In case there is anything that you are not comfortable with, for instance, physically, you should never compromise. You, your safety, and your values should be off-limits when it comes to compromising. Being able to take care of yourself needs to come before making your partner happy when both of you are in conflict with each other.

THERE IS NO NEED TO BE "RIGHT" ALL THE TIME

It might be exhilarating to walk away from any argument with your partner having the last word. Although this could feel gratifying, looking at fights in regard to who is wrong and who is right is a harmful approach. The primary goal of a relationship is to understand one another all the time. Try to listen to your partner actively. Try to understand why their point of view is so important to them. In place of trying to convince them of your opinion loudly, consider whether there are various good or right outcomes to be reached.

NEGOTIATING A TRADE

By looking at its nature, a compromise never indicates all or nothing. However, it also does not indicate that you should never allow your partner to get their way completely. In case you cannot find common ground on one problem, try to negotiate a trade so that both of you can get something you want. For instance, if your partner desires to see the latest thriller, ask them if you can choose where you will have dinner. You will have to be open to your partner's side of the trade-off. To make a compromise successful, both people are required to feel good about the same.

GIVING YOUR BEST TO FIND COMMON GROUND

In your effort to reach a compromise, it might feel that both you and your partner have no common ground. However, you will have to do your best to determine something that both of you can agree with. It does not matter, even when it is not the main point of discussion. For the majority of the time, when any couple argues, they try to listen for all that is wrong in what their partners are trying to say. Then, they want to clarify, debate, or correct what is being said. Such a mindset can rarely get both of you what you want. So, in place of doing so, try to listen with the intention of finding something that you can agree with. For instance, when you argue about who needs to clean the dishes, take some time to acknowledge how great it is that both of you want a clean kitchen.

ENSURING TO STAY CALM

You will have to ensure that you compromise from a calm state of mind. It is one of the easiest things to get heated when you disagree with your partner regarding something. However, an emotional state of this kind can make things harder to get to a middle ground. You will have to understand that when you get emotionally activated, you lose perspective. So, take the time you require before starting a conversation to go for a walk, meditate, shower, and so on. As both of you get centered and feel that you are set to work together as a team to find a solution, you can go ahead and start working things out.

SELECTING YOUR BATTLES

It is not possible to be in a relationship on your terms. Although wanting everything to go as per your preferences might seem ideal, that cannot be regarded to be realistic.

So, it is necessary to select your battles. Everything can never go your way in a relationship. Decide all those things that are most important to you to concentrate on to determine the middle ground. For instance, if allowing your partner to select the wall color of the living room is not a big deal for you, try to convince them of that. When something is extremely important to you, you can have more leverage.

LISTENING INTENTLY

When you try to compromise with your partner, the main concern might be to get the points across in a compelling and rational way. However, in order to attain an effective middle ground, listening can be regarded as the key. Try to listen to the views of your partner on the topic and genuinely listen to them.

It is possible that as you see things from their perspective and understand how they feel about it, you might start to feel differently. In place of trying to prepare your counter-argument in your mind as your partner speaks, try to consider what they are saying. It will help in making sure that both of you understand each other in a better way.

TRYING BOTH WAYS

When you and your partner try to reach a compromise, you might not be able to try both of your suggestions all the time. For instance, when both of you have differing opinions regarding which dog to adopt, you cannot bring home both and return one later. However, this tip can be useful for various other situations. In case you argue about the perfect park to have a picnic, you can plan two picnics. It can ensure that you can compare which one is the most fun.

You can try it both ways for a short period. Although doing so would not win one of you over, it can be useful to experience a trial run to find out what can actually work the best for you two.

MAPPING OUT PRIORITIES

In case trying to reach a compromise with the help of discussion is not getting you anywhere, you can take things to paper. Both of you will need to draw a circle on a piece of paper, with a small circle in the middle of the bigger one. You will identify your core needs in the small circle – all those things that are inflexible. In the larger circle, note down the areas where you are ready to be flexible.
The exercise can help both of you understand each other's point of view in a better way.

You will also get to understand each other's boundaries, and it can show you ways to compromise.

Regardless of the problem that is trying to cause tension in your relationship, it is necessary to show each other love with the help of compromise. Arguments might turn out to be nasty.

However, when you successfully keep the discussion respectful and kind, it can actually go a long way for the relationship. But ensure that you are aware of the toxic traits of your partner before you get ready to compromise on things.

CHAPTER 3
REDUCE RELATIONSHIP CONFLICTS

Every couple experiences conflict at one time or the other. Conflict can never be regarded as bad all the time. When two individuals get into a relationship, conflict resolution is an important skill to learn so that you can deal with conflicts whenever they arise. Arguments develop when the needs or wants of one partner are not being met. So, whenever you experience conflict, it could be a sign that the relationship is required to grow. However, unresolved conflicts in a relationship are not at all healthy. This is especially the case when conflicts define the relationship with tense and chaotic energy. It is necessary to resolve conflicts so that you can feel safe and ensure that the relationship can thrive.

BEING DIRECT

Most often, people do not come out and state all that tends to bother them. We try to opt for indirect ways to express displeasure. A partner might speak to the other in a way that implies underlying hostility. Couples might also try to avoid discussing problems by switching topics when the problem arises. Expressing anger in such indirect ways cannot be regarded as constructive as they can never give the target of the behavior a proper idea regarding how to respond. You might be aware of the fact that your partner is irritated. However, the lack of directness can leave you with no form of guidance regarding what to do to solve the issue.

STOP BEING PASSIVE-AGGRESSIVE

In case you try to suppress anger when you are angry at your family members or partner, it might turn out to be unhealthy. Not talking to your partner when you get angry can be regarded as a no-win strategy. However, most people still try to do it. You might try to do it so that you can stay away from conflicts. However, with time, it ends up developing resentment between you two. It can prolong the argument. Glaring at your partner and expecting them to understand why you are angry is never going to work. All it will do is make them feel punished, angrier, or confused. As you manage conflict, it is necessary to have some faith in the other individual. You will have to share what you feel in an honest way so that your partner gets to understand your point of view. Try to set rules to fight fair right at the start of the relationship. Stay away from silent treatment, never go to bed angry, and listen with judgments.

SLOWING DOWN DISCUSSIONS

It is suggested to slow down and stick to one problem at a time. When you get triggered by negative patterns making you feel angry and frustrated, it might get hard to keep track of all that is being said. It is because the discussion will move quickly, and before you can be aware of it, multiple problems are being opened at once. An effective way of taking care of conflicts is to spend some time slowing down the process so that you get to listen to what your partner is saying. Take the necessary time to reflect on each other's perspectives right before you decide to respond.

CHOOSING YOUR WORDS

All your words start in the form of thoughts and slowly turn into actions. When a partner tends to make personal attacks with sarcastic tones, ugly curses, or name-calling, the impact on the relationship is going to be huge. You will have to try to communicate in a healthy way by selecting your words with utmost care. Also, pause in the middle of an argument to breathe. If you keep shooting out negative words, it is going to make your life less happy and less interesting, besides dampening the relationship potential. When you choose kind words, you can get to hear the same in return as well.

LETTING GO OF THE PAST

There is no doubt that constantly trying to hold onto the past can hurt. As you keep dwelling on them, their power over you will increase. Never keep a tally of who won which argument in your relationship. It has no point at all. Try to bring all your attention to the current moment, to the position where your relationship is right now. Give your best to free the relationship from the baggage of the last argument or fight. It can be regarded as an important aspect of moving your relationship toward a healthy future.

QUICK REPAIR TO BE BACK ON TRACK

Right after you have a fight, whether it is a cyclone or a mild one, the primary step is to repair the relationship as soon as possible. It involves taking responsibility and apologizing for the hurt. It might be the case that you and your partner were not able to solve the conflict before going to sleep. So, you slept in different beds due to this. The first thing that you will have to do in the morning is sit down and talk. It is never a good idea to go off to work while being mad at each other.

Unsolved conflicts will hamper both of you. Forgiveness can get easier each time you do it. Couples who resolve conflicts as soon as they can make a lifelong team. They can get back on track easily. With time, this can foster ongoing resilience in a relationship.

TALK ABOUT YOUR FEELINGS WITHOUT BLAMING YOUR PARTNER

All those statements that tend to assault your partner's character directly can be extremely harmful to your relationship. For instance, when a person who is frustrated by the jealousy of their partner says, "You are not at all rational," it is nothing more than inviting the jealous partner to be defensive. It can easily shut down any sort of future conversation. You can opt for a constructive strategy like using an "I statement." You can also pair them with behavioral descriptions. I statement always pay attention to the way you feel, without any need to blame your partner. Behavior description focuses on a particular behavior that your partner might be engaging in instead of a character flaw. For instance, the person from the above-mentioned example could say, "I get irritated when you say I am trying to flirt with someone while having an innocent conversation." Such tactics are direct in nature and will never point at the character of your partner.

OPTING FOR A DIFFERENT PERSPECTIVE

Besides trying to listen to your partner, you will also have to take their perspective and understand where they are actually coming from. People who are able to take the perspective of their partner have fewer chances of getting angry in the time of conflict discussion. It has been found that being able to take a more objective perspective can be useful. When you try to opt for the perspective of your partner, you can easily understand their side of the story. It will make things easier for you to get to a middle ground.

DO NOT OBJECT TO YOUR PARTNER'S COMPLAINTS AUTOMATICALLY

As you get criticized, it could be a hard thing not to get defensive. However, you will have to understand that defensiveness can never help in solving problems. Think of a couple arguing as the wife wants the husband to take care of more household chores. When she asks him to do a quick clean-up as he prepares to leave for work, he says, "I do not have time for this in the morning. When the wife asks to set aside time on the weekend, he says, "But we have plans on the weekend, and I need to fulfill those. So, I don't think that would work." Such kind of "yes-but" behavior can indicate that her ideas are not at all important. Another common and destructive behavior is "cross-complaining" as you respond to the complaint of your partner with something of your own. For instance, responding to "You never clean the house" with "You are a clean freak." It is necessary to listen to your partner and consider what they are trying to say.

NEVER SAY NEVER

As you try to address a problem, you need to stay away from making generalizations about your partner. Certain statements such as, "You never help me with household chores" or "You keep staring at your phone" are most likely to make your partner get defensive. Instead of trying to prompt a discussion regarding how your partner can be more attentive or helpful, it would make your partner generate counterexamples as to when they were. Making your partner defensive is never going to help the relationship.

DO NOT SHOW CONTEMPT FOR YOUR PARTNER

Out of all kinds of negative things that can be done and said at the time of a conflict, the worst might be contempt. Contemptuous are all those remarks that tend to belittle someone. It might involve name-calling and sarcasm. Also, it might include nonverbal behavior such as smirking or rolling eyes. The behavior of this kind is disrespectful. It is an implication that you are disgusted with your partner. Suppose one partner says, "I wish we could go out more," and the other partner says, "Yes, what is more important for you is to overpay for tiny portions of food. Could you be more superficial?" Contempt of this sort can make it impossible to strike up a real conversation. In fact, the chances are high that you will make your partner angry in place of solving the issue.

BEING AWARE OF TAKING A TIME-OUT

In case you find yourself falling into negative patterns and determine that neither of you is following the above-mentioned tips, you need to take a time-out from your argument. Even opting for a few deep breaths could be enough to calm down hot tempers. Airing all your grievances could be useful or productive for the relationship. However, conflicts are required to be managed skillfully so that you can stop them from getting worse.

CHAPTER 4
NARCISSISTIC CONTROL TACTICS

You will come across people who will walk up to you and smile as they greet you. They will act in a way as if they love you. In fact, they might pretend to be your best friend or loving family. However, the truth is that they have bad intentions regarding you, and their act of being friendly is nothing more than an act. When you are aware of the patterns and signs of narcissism, you can pick up the deception cues and regard them to be what they are – control tactics. Manipulation can be regarded as a kind of emotional blackmail. Manipulators might use certain behaviors to influence the way in which you perceive them. In fact, they might use such tactics to influence the way you feel, think, and act.

For instance, they might try to act sickly so that they can paint themselves as innocent and vulnerable. But when you are not looking, they will give their best to wreak havoc on your emotional and mental well-being. When you get alarmed by your gut instincts that someone has got wrong intentions, you need to take necessary action to protect yourself. None of us have got control over how others behave or whether other people like us or not. They will conspire and plot when that is all they desire to do. You are the one to decide whether to stop it or not. You will have to pay attention to signs of manipulation. Whenever you spot them getting used against you, remove yourself from the situation.

Short-term or long-term manipulative relationships are traumatizing and abusive. But the sad news is that victims of such abuse are mostly blind to manipulation. You might find it hard to consider that people who claim to cherish and love you do not have your best interests. They are utilizing psychological control to hamper your success and happiness. It does not matter who the manipulator is; when you are in an abusive relationship, you need to get yourself to safety. You might accept this later, but manipulators and narcissists never change. Let's have a look at some of the control tactics used by narcissists.

SHOWER YOU WITH ATTENTION

Narcissists will try to shower you with attention and gifts. They might also pretend to be happy as they get to see you. But in reality, they will plan for your downfall. Manipulators are mostly sweet talkers. They utilize flattery to win over. They might get you small gifts and make huge public displays by presenting them to you. All they want is to show others how much they care for you. It might get confusing for you as you will not be able to see past the charm of their seduction. Narcissists can make you feel seen and understood. It can develop a fake feeling of intimacy.

GASLIGHTING

When you get gaslighted, you will feel uncomfortable. You can sense that something wrong occurred, but the narcissist in your life will tell you that nothing happened. You imagined everything, and you are nothing more than crazy.

In simple terms, you are lied to, and that can make you doubt yourself. Gaslighting is often regarded as the most insidious tactic used by narcissists to take control. As you keep doubting yourself, it will slowly change your sense of reality. Self-doubt can eat away the ability to have faith in yourself. As a result, you will not be able to call out mistreatment and abuse.

To deal with this, you can note down events to have a record for later usage. You can have a group of trusted relations you can share all the information with. Having a trusted group can validate what happened.

PROJECTION OF NEGATIVE FEELINGS

Projection is more like a defense mechanism used by narcissists to displace responsibility for all their negative traits and behaviors. They do so by attributing the same to someone else. One thing you need to be aware of is that narcissists can never bear to think of themselves as bad, difficult, or responsible for anything. They keep projecting feelings that they cannot take care of outwards instead of moving them inward. In simple terms, they can never own up to what they have done. It can be said that they create their own world. In their world, everything seems to revolve around them. Everyone else in their life plays the role of serving them and their purposes. "You are sulking and ruining my day. You are mad," for instance, are some of the things they might say to keep you off the center.

Projection is when a narcissistic individual dumps their traits on others. In place of trying to admit that self-improvement might be necessary, they expect others to take care of their bad behaviors. Detaching from such connections is the best solution. If you feel sorry for them, deny the charge, or try to explain yourself, you will end up opening further ways of manipulation.

MISREPRESENTATION OF OPINIONS, FEELINGS, AND THOUGHTS

Remember that narcissists are experts in reading minds. Toxic personalities assume that they are aware of what you are feeling and thinking. All of their triggers drive the reactions. They never tend to evaluate what is actually happening. They will try to put words in your mouth. In fact, you might get accused of thinking of them to be toxic. Narcissists can reframe all that you say so that they can make your opinions seem absurd. Suppose you bring up the fact that you are not happy with how your toxic partner is speaking to you. In response, they might say, "You mean to say you are perfect?" or "You are indicating that I am the bad one here?" It makes them take away your right to have emotions and thoughts regarding inappropriate behaviors. They will make you feel guilty as you try to develop boundaries.

If you say, "I never said that," and walk away, it can help in setting up a firm boundary in such interactions. As long as the blame-shifting of a narcissist works, no focus will be given to their behavior.

ALTERING THE SUBJECT

It is another smokescreen tactic used by narcissists. The tactic can help in diverting a conversation regarding what a narcissist did in some other direction. Generally, the redirection will land on your weaknesses. Narcissistic people would never want you to hold them accountable for anything. Trying to complain about their actions or behaviors? They will end up pointing out a mistake that you made ten years ago. Diversion of this kind has got no limits in regard to subject content or time. Generally, this kind of diversion starts with a sentence such as, "Do you remember the time when…." Keep in mind that diversions are required to be redirected to the original subject. You can say, "That is not at all what I am talking about. Please pay attention to the actual issue." In case the broken record keeps focusing on you, disengage and try to spend your energy on something constructive. There is no meaning in debating with someone who possesses the mind of a toddler.

TRIANGULATION

Triangulation is about bringing the perspective, opinion, or threat of someone else into the relationship dynamic. Narcissists of malignant nature are fond of triangulating their partners with ex-partners, colleagues, friends, strangers, and even family members to bolster the claims. When a narcissist alters the story to make you look like the aggressor, it helps in validating their abuse. But at the same time, it will invalidate your reaction to the abuse. The act of triangulation can put you on the defensive mode, besides making things hard for other people to understand what is going on. In case you try to defend yourself vigorously, that might also end up validating the claims of the other person.

Triangulation often creates love triangles that can leave you on the outside, making you feel insecure and unhinged. Narcissists might also utilize the opinions of other people so that they can validate their point of view. It can be regarded as a diversionary tactic that is meant to pull your attention away from all kinds of abusive behaviors. It can create a false image of the narcissist as a desirable person. It might leave you questioning yourself – when Thomas agreed with Henry, does not that indicate you are wrong? But in reality, narcissists love to report back falsehoods about what other people say about you when they are the ones smearing you.

In order to resist the tactics of triangulation, you will have to understand that whoever the narcissist is triangulating with is also the person who is getting triangulated by your relationship with the narcissistic person as well. In simple terms, everyone gets played by this one individual. You can reverse-triangulate the narcissist by getting support from a person who is not under the influence of the narcissist. Also, this can be done by seeking your own validation.

SMEARING AND STALKING

Narcissists might slander you and report back to people who are close to you, their loved ones, or anyone who will listen to them. They create stories that will present you as abusive. They will pretend to be the victims of abuse. Your narcissistic partner might claim that you engage in all those behaviors that they do not want to be accused of. In fact, they might intentionally make you angry so that the angry reactions can be used against you.

Such activities can sabotage your reputation and slander your name so that you get no support system to fall back on when you detach and cut ties. In such situations, you need to get help. There is no need to wait until things go too far. Try to stick to the facts and try not to react when you get used as an object of a smear campaign.

CHAPTER 5
DETERMINING TOXICITY IN A RELATIONSHIP

A toxic relationship is a kind of partnership that involves activities on the part of a toxic partner that is physically and emotionally hurtful. It does not indicate that toxic people in a relationship are life-threatening and physically destructive.

However, a toxic relationship might simply mean that the other individual feels threatened, scared, and terrified to provide their thoughts. It is mainly because of the fact that they are afraid and worried about the emotional responses of the toxic partner.

When you are in a good relationship, you feel respected, cared for, heard, and protected. But when you are in a dysfunctional relationship, all such elements will be absent. In a healthy relationship, everything appears to work or get sorted out easily. It is not an indication that good relationships do not have arguments.
However, arguments are handled in the right way, besides making you feel that you are heading in the right direction. In a toxic relationship, everything might seem like a trigger to start a quarrel. Also, there will be no ending to the disagreements.

So, you are most likely to get locked in a war cycle.

Types of Toxic Partners

If you want to determine toxicity in a relationship, you will have to understand the types of toxic relationships. Even successful relationships might have minor periods of actions that can be called to be toxic. After all, human beings are not flawless. We learn as we go. All that differentiates a toxic relationship is dysfunction as the norm. To the external world, the toxic partner acts in an excellent way. Toxic individuals act in the way they do for a reason – they need to be in control besides having all the power in the relationship. In a toxic relationship, power sharing is like a dream. It is true that power clashes are common in every relationship, but toxic partners insist on being in charge.

- **Belittler:** A toxic person of this kind will keep belittling you. They will tend to make fun of you all the time, besides making you believe that your goals or views are worthless. In fact, they might not think twice before degrading you in public.

- **Hot tempered:** Controlling with the help of intimidation is regarded as a characteristic habit of a toxic partner. Such people tend to have temper issues. A small mistake and their anger flares up.

- **Dependent:** A toxic partner of this kind will always be intentionally dependent on the other. A toxic partner might be so passive that you end up making all their choices.

- **The user:** Users, especially at the start of the relationship, will appear to be respectful and lovely. They will be so as long as they keep getting all they want.

- **Guilt-inducer:** A guilt-inducer will try their best to dominate you by making you feel bad every time you do something they don't like. They can make you do things simply by making you feel guilty.

Toxic Relationship and Its Signs

Now that you are aware of the types of toxic partners, let's look at some of the signs of toxicity to determine whether you are in a toxic relationship.

NO SUPPORT

Healthy relationships need to be based on a mutual desire to see each other succeed in every aspect of life. However, when things turn out to be toxic, all kinds of achievements slowly take the shape of a competition. In simple terms, the time that you dedicate to spending with each other does not feel positive. You lack encouragement or support from the relationship. In fact, you can no longer trust your partner to show up for you. You might also get the impression that your interests and needs do not even matter and that your partner only cares about what they desire.

JEALOUSY OR ENVY

Although it is okay to experience a bit of envy from time to time, it might turn out to be an issue when the envy of your partner keeps you away from thinking positively about all your successes. The same thing can be applied to jealousy.

Jealousy is a natural human emotion. However, the moment it results in continuous mistrust and suspicion, it can start eroding the base of the relationship.

TOXIC COMMUNICATION

In place of mutual respect and kindness, when the majority of your conversations are stuffed with criticism or sarcasm besides being fueled by contempt, it is a predictor of toxicity in your relationship. Do you find your partner making remarks to you or your actions? Maybe they repeat all that you said in a mocking tone from another room. In that case, you might even start to dodge their calls to get a break from the arguments.

CONTROLLING BEHAVIORS

Is it the habit of your partner to keep asking you where you are all the time? Or it might be the case that they get irritated or annoyed when you fail to answer their texts or receive their calls immediately. Behaviors of this kind are most likely to stem from a lack of trust or jealousy. But these signs or behaviors might also indicate a requirement for control. In certain cases, the attempts to control might end up being abuse.

DISHONESTY

When your partner makes up lies about their whereabouts or who they meet with, it is a sign of toxicity in your relationship. A healthy relationship is one when both partners can be completely honest with each other. There is no place for dishonesty in a healthy relationship.

FEELING BAD ALL THE TIME

You go to sleep feeling hollow, and you wake up the same. You see other couples doing happy couple things, and you can feel the sting. Why are you not able to feel the same sort of love? When you stay in a toxic relationship for a long time, it can eat away your confidence and courage, making you feel bad all the time.

ALL THE WORK COMES FROM YOU

It is not possible to hold a relationship when you are the one who does all the work. It can be exhausting and lonely. In case you cannot leave the relationship, give what you are required to give. But make sure that you do not give anything more than that. You will have to get rid of the fantasy that you can improve things if you try hard.

DEFLECTION

When you try to tell your partner that you are hurt, angry, or unhappy regarding something they have done and find yourself taking care of their unhappiness or anger, your partner is an overreactor or deflector. You might find yourself comforting him/her in place of taking care of yourself. In fact, you might feel selfish as you brought up something that ended up upsetting your partner. Your initial hurt or anger gets lost as you look after the feelings of your partner.

THE VICTIM CARD

When your partner always tries to use the victim card, it can slowly result in a lack of communication. They will blame you for your sufferings besides making themselves the victim. Being in a relationship with a person who is unable to recognize their shortcomings can make progress impossible.

YOU FEEL RELIEVED ALONE

It is normal and healthy to have alone time. Also, it can make you appreciate your partner even more when you are not around them all the time. However, you might not be in a healthy relationship when you always desire to escape their company. In case you do feel this way, question yourself, "Why?" It could be the case that your partner is adding extra stress to your life, or they do not give you enough space. In a healthy relationship, you should want to be with your partner a lot more than you want to be alone.

NOTHING GETS RESOLVED

Every relationship experiences issues. However, when you are in a toxic relationship, nothing seems to work out, as every conflict tends to end in an argument. There is a lack of trust that your partner will have the power to handle the problem in a way that can preserve the connection. As this happens, needs tend to get buried. Unmet needs in a relationship will lead to resentment.

Toxic behavioral patterns and communication can corrode the foundation of a relationship. However, there is no need to stand by and watch the bond with your partner crumble. If things tend to go out of hand, you can take the help of a relationship therapist. But there is no meaning in staying in a relationship where you end up losing your true self as you get filled with stress and hurt due to the toxic behaviors of your partner.

CHAPTER 6
NARCISSISTIC ABUSE

Narcissistic abuse is a kind of emotional abuse where an abuser only tends to think about themselves. They might end up using actions and words to manipulate the behavior and emotional state of their partner. The overall effects of narcissistic abuse might vary based on how long a person can deal with such relationships. The effects tend to range from mild to severe, with some of the survivors recovering with time and others might have to deal with lifelong damage. Let us have a look at some of the ways in which narcissistic abuse can hamper your life.

ANXIETY

Most survivors of narcissistic abuse end up living with anxiety. As you experience narcissistic abuse, you are most likely to experience anxiety or fear while trying to be in relationships with new people. People who run away from abusive relationships might experience separation anxiety. It can make them feel disoriented and panicked when they are far away from the abusers. In case your symptoms include panic attacks, anxiety attacks, or hypervigilance right after being abused by a narcissist, understand that the symptoms will ease with time. It is especially the case when you can work through the trauma with the help of a professional.

POST-TRAUMATIC STRESS

As you survive narcissistic abuse, you might experience symptoms of post-traumatic stress. The brain will be on high alert, always being wary of danger. It is because the traumatic events ended up triggering a fight or flight response inside you. Due to this, anything that is linked with all the abusive memories can trigger an anxiety attack. After getting out of an abusive relationship, you might feel the requirement to be on guard all the time. Narcissistic abuse victims often mention having no idea what their abusive partner would do next. You might find it tough to relax due to hypervigilance. In fact, you might try to steer clear of some things or situations that remind you of the abuse. It could range from avoiding certain people or certain places.

DEPRESSION

People who experience narcissistic abuse might also develop depression. Abuse survivors often deal with feelings of worthlessness after years of being told how useless they are by their abuser. After a long time of being gaslighted and manipulated, you might also end up isolating yourself. It can make your feelings of depression even worse.

NO SENSE OF SELF AND SELF-WORTH

You might feel as if you have lost yourself completely. Narcissistic abuse can be regarded as a kind of brainwashing. So, it has a high chance of destroying your sense of self-worth. In fact, you might not be able to feel like the person you were before all the abuse began. In certain cases, people who experience narcissistic abuse might find it hard to recognize themselves in the mirror. It is because they can no longer see their true reflection who is staring back at them. Also, you might have trust issues with others and find yourself second-guessing yourself. You might start feeling that you are not good enough or that you are the one who did something to lead to the abuse in the first place. It can result in embarrassment and shame. As a result, it can prevent you from getting the necessary help. You might not be able to make decisions. Simple decisions might seem like a big deal for you.

COGNITIVE ISSUES

After narcissistic abuse, it might get hard for you to focus on daily tasks, like completing household chores or even watching TV. The memories of all the traumatic events are regarded to interfere with focus and concentration. You might even experience memory loss, which is mostly short-term. It is due to the fact that the brain releases lots of stress hormones when it gets traumatized. It affects the hippocampus area of the brain.

INABILITY TO FORGIVE YOURSELF

Many narcissistic abuse victims tend to struggle with feeling unworthy or even believe that they deserve the way the abuser treated them. It might seem like there is something wrong with you when a person who was supposed to love you used such cruel powers against you. You might have to deal with low levels of self-esteem. You might get the thought that the abuser would have treated you in a better way if you could have done things in a different way. Focusing on dreams and goals might seem like a problem as well. It might be because you stay preoccupied with the thoughts of all that happened to you. In extreme cases, your self-worth might get so damaged that you find it hard to believe that good things can take place in your life.

PHYSICAL SYMPTOMS

Physical symptoms like stomach aches, headaches, or body aches are quite common after you experience narcissistic abuse. You might find it tough to fall asleep and cannot shut off your brain at night as you stay stressed regarding what happened. In fact, you might experience nightmares that could haunt you for several days.

EMOTIONAL LABILITY

After experiencing episodes of traumatic events like narcissistic abuse, it is quite natural to suffer from mood swings along with excessive irritability. You might start acting like a robot who has no emotion at all. In some cases, abusers might experience depersonalization, where they feel nothing is right around them.

TRUST ISSUES

Your trust levels are most likely to be low as you get out of narcissistic abuse. Although this might seem like a good thing, it might end up hindering all your future relationships. In fact, it is such an issue that it might result in other problems like social anxiety. You might find yourself wondering all the time whether others around you are being truthful with you or if they are trying to manipulate your emotions to get what they desire. You might get overly sensitive to judgment or criticism from others because you will be scared of being betrayed again.

You might have to deal with trust issues in every aspect of life. It also includes your friendships, personal relationships, and work interactions. Keep in mind that as you get out of an abusive relationship, your abusive partner might try to contact you. It can keep you stuck in the constant cycle of abuse.

SELF-DESTRUCTIVE HABITS

A common effect of narcissistic abuse is self-destructive habits. All those who have been in relationships with narcissists often get the feeling of punishing themselves. It is because they feel they are the ones at fault for the bad behaviors of their partners towards them. You might have to deal with addiction issues like smoking, drinking, or food addiction. All such addictions are nothing more than ways to numb the emotional pain.

PEOPLE PLEASING

You might turn into a people pleaser and give your best to make others like you. You might get overly accommodating so that you can get approval from other people after walking on eggshells for a long time. It might be the case that you are not able to express your thoughts and emotions as you have a fear of getting judged for anything you say. In order to avoid confrontation with a narcissist, you develop the habit of bottling up all your feelings.

HEALING FROM NARCISSISTIC ABUSE

Narcissistic abuse is powerful enough to destroy the foundation of the life of most people. It takes energy and time to heal from the heartbreak, betrayal, financial losses, and gaslighting caused by an abuser. In fact, you might lose family members and friends along the way because of self-isolation. In case you are struggling, it is necessary to learn the ways in which you can heal. Let us have a look at some of the ways in which you can heal from narcissistic abuse.

- **Educating yourself:** Try to figure out the traits of a narcissist and what is involved in narcissistic abuse so that you can recognize when you are getting manipulated.

- **Recognizing and accepting your feelings:** You are most likely to experience various kinds of emotions like depression, grief, anxiety, and anger. No matter what you feel, it is valid. It is necessary not to suppress any of your feelings or end up judging yourself as you have them.

- **Joining a support group:** There are several communities online and in real life for all those who experienced the same kind of abuse. You can find it helpful to interact with other people who can understand what you experienced. In fact, you can get advice and coping tips.

- **Self-care:** When the level of self-esteem touches the base, it is quite natural to feel that you do not deserve anything good in life or for yourself. But it is important to take care of yourself. You need to ensure that you get enough sleep, engage in activities that can make you happy, and eat healthy food.

- **Reaching out to a therapist:** A therapist can provide you with all the necessary tools that you will require to heal from the effects of narcissistic abuse in a safe space.

As you get involved with a narcissistic partner, you might develop one or more of the above-mentioned effects.
You might end up developing some coping mechanisms that are negative in nature. You will have to understand that dealing with a narcissist is not that easy. It is necessary to take care of yourself in the first place before you can deal with them.

A narcissist might make your life seem like hell. However, being aware of the signs in advance can help you stay out of their reach.

CHAPTER 7
STARTING THE HEALING PROCESS

Every person's experience of healing is unique. Even though it isn't always simple, opting to quit a toxic relationship might be the wisest course of action. When there has been trauma or toxicity in the relationship, it may be very difficult to recover. The process of healing comes next if you're considering ending. Being involved in a toxic relationship has serious repercussions. Your mental health suffers, and it causes melancholy, anxiety, and insecurities.

So because the chain of toxicity becomes addicting over time, it does seem impossible to break free of it. Several victims of narcissistic abuse feel like they will never be able to heal from a toxic relationship, and there are many reasons for this. Every person's experience of healing is unique.

How to Start the Healing Process

It's possible for the unfavorable dynamics and attitudes we encounter to stick to our minds and continue to have an impact on us years later. In toxic relationships, our thoughts are frequently the worst captives. However, that does not imply that we will always remain somewhat free. Even while the job has never been quick or simple, it may be quite rewarding. The following stage of emancipation could be greatly assisted by the following principles.

- **Don't be too hard on yourself:** Understand that training your brain requires a while. You're still developing. Childhood messages could stick with you for a very long time. The patterns you developed from your toxic relationship, though it occurred in adulthood and only lasted a short while, could be challenging to change. Whenever you realize that now the toxic relationship is still influencing your thoughts and behavior, be kind to yourself. Giving yourself the space or time to recover rather than just being irritated with yourself only serves to reinforce the toxic attitude.

- **Make a note of your self-talk:** Watch out for what your inner voice is trying to tell you. As you investigate the connections in your mind, be inquisitive like a researcher. It's necessary that you record the ideas you come up with in writing. It is more useful to write down your ideas than it is to just mentally record them. It will be much easier for you to begin forming more beneficial ways of thinking.

- **Use a gentler tone of voice:** Start bringing more uplifting thoughts in to replace your judgmental and harsh ones. Not certain what to say? Think about the language you use to address a close friend or use to address a close friend or your child. Be gentle while responding when you notice that you are still talking to yourself in the same manner. For instance, instead of saying, "You are a fool!" say, "Everyone makes this type of mistake."

- **Recognize your strengths:** Increase your participation in the things that make you feel alive and in which you excel. Because manipulative people often do not want to see you succeed, you might have decided to give up those activities throughout your toxic relationship. A potent remedy is being aware of your expertise.

- **Accept who you are:** We frequently hide or ignore significant aspects of ourselves as a result of toxic relationships. For instance, if your parents were always judgmental of you, you might well have hidden your natural excitement. Find periods of silence and use them to hear what needs to be said. Look within to see if you are suppressing any urges. Start clearing more room for your adventure.

- **Make your schedule simpler:** Make conscious room for the activities that you believe will add worth to your life. Consider engaging in some energizing physical activity. Breathe deeply and visualize having a sharp consciousness of your body, thoughts, and emotions. Writing down your thoughts will help you mentally let go of all the negative things that are piling up in your head. Don't be hesitant to record your experiences in writing.

Tips on How to Get Over a Toxic Relationship

Keep these basic tips in mind as you move on from an emotionally draining relationship so that you can heal yourself from the effects of a toxic relationship.

- **Don't expect closure:** Maybe you'd like to keep the lines of contact open with your ex because you want to get closure via apologies from them. Sometimes it can be draining to wait around for a heartfelt apology that, in some situations, might not ever arrive. Most of the time, the healing work that survivors accomplish within themselves will provide the closure that a lot of them seek instead of the toxic ex.

- **Keep a strong support system of positive individuals:** Ensure that you are surrounded by positive individuals. Relatives, colleagues, psychotherapists, support groups, and other people can all be part of a support system. It may be very helpful to be able to spend some time with a person whom you trust and with whom you have a solid relationship. This is the moment to get back in touch with your inner group or establish new pals because toxic relationships have such a tendency to keep people apart. Additionally, they will be a great source of support for you when you are down and inclined to contact your ex. If you want a pick-me-up and you are sad, talk to them instead.

- **Set firm boundaries:** Relationships that are toxic lack reciprocity. For instance, your narcissistic partner may disregard your limits because they believe you exist only to serve their wants. Define clear personal boundaries if you must continue to interact with a toxic individual (for example, if you both have children in common). Inform them of the behaviors you won't allow while maintaining your composure and being tough and consistent.

- **Realize that you deserve healthy love:** You must not let your negative relationship experiences lead you to assume that you are unworthy of happiness and happy partnerships. Keep in mind that everyone in the world is worthy of love. Regardless of whatever happens, always have faith in yourself since recognizing your value can be the only way to attract people who feel the same way.

- **Try not to "check-in" with your former partner:** It might be very alluring to want to get in touch with your ex after going through a toxic relationship, particularly one that lasted a long time. But it's frequently preferable to allow yourself some space and avoid all communication. You may be lured back into the harmful tango if you're in communication with your ex. Regardless of what they might claim, you don't have to keep in touch with this person or be friends with them. There are beneficial ways for co-parenting with such a person who is difficult to interact with if there are kids involved because contact will inevitably occur. I will discuss this in detail in the next chapter.

- **Recognize your feelings:** It's difficult to decide to end a toxic relationship. Despite the sensation of freedom you have, it triggers unpleasant and perplexing emotions. You must therefore comprehend your feelings. Let yourself experience all of your feelings, including anger, sadness, and joy. Try not to suppress them because doing so delays recovery. Being in pain does not imply weakness. Rather, it aids in the processing of your feelings and gives you the willpower to let go.

- **Avoid rushing into a new relationship:** Before returning, give yourself time to recover to prevent a rebound. Pause your dating activities, reflect, and assess your existing situation.

- **Confidence-boosting decisions:** The main reason a toxic relationship denigrates you or treats you like nothing is that they believe you would perish without them. Increase your knowledge of the things you shied away from since you were too fearful and shy to do them. Create a sense of accomplishment by setting goals and objectives to take on and finish modest activities before moving on to bigger ones to feel independent. You are accountable for anything in your life that needs repairing or replacing, including your financial obligations, your work, your physical well-being, and so forth. Once you start working on your own, you'll feel a lot better and more self-assured.

It can be challenging to move on from a toxic relationship. However, being able to spot toxicity earlier on and make plans accordingly will increase your confidence when it comes to ending things with your significant other or the toxic person. Don't put off taking action any longer; it's necessary to place your well-being and health first when coping with any kind of toxic relationship.

Therefore, if you're interacting with someone who saps your happiness and strength, think about cutting them out of your life or seek immediate help if you are the victim of physical or emotional abuse.

CHAPTER 8
IMPORTANCE OF NO CONTACT

It may sound harsh advice to tell someone, "Don't call them," after you've decided to end a toxic relationship, but there are situations when staying out of contact with your ex is the wisest course of action. *The no-contact rule enters the picture here.* Keeping in touch with your ex makes reconciliation more likely. You might be subjected to emotional blackmail by toxic people who are skilled at manipulating your emotions. Unless you have children together and must co-parent, stop all contact with your partner as soon as it is ready to split up. If so, only talk to each other about the kids. This no-contact rule is pretty self-explanatory - you are not allowed to contact your toxic ex for a predetermined amount of time, usually between 30 to 45 days. The no-contact strategy is important for you in letting go of your toxic partner.

No Contact: What It Is and What It Isn't

No Contact (NC) is neither a game nor a way to trick someone into coming back into your life; numerous dating books, including websites, have misunderstood this tactic.

We shouldn't wish for those who have harmed us to re-enter our lives. No Contact is just the key that seals out that toxic person from ever re-entering our heart, thoughts, and spirit in any tangible form, allowing us to enjoy life, healthier lives while nurturing our real selves and minimizing people-pleasing.

This phrase is frequently used in regard to narcissistic relationships. In a relationship with a narcissist or any emotionally abusive individual, you eventually understand why cutting off communication is advised. Your thoughts begin to clear, and you start to feel relieved once you decide to cease interacting with the toxic individual.

TYPES OF NO-CONTACT RULES

Every person is unique, and this includes the connections they maintain. Consequently, it is practically impossible to establish a universal no-contact policy. Here are the several categories of no-contact rules that you could adhere to depending on your individual circumstances.

- **The standard no-contact policy:** After a split, the usual no-contact rule applies, as was previously discussed. This rule prohibits you from contacting your ex through any channel for a specified period of time.

- **The limited no-contact rule:** This rule states that you may only have brief interactions with your ex-partner in unavoidable situations. If you and your partner have mutual financial obligations, like a loan, you might abide by this regulation. If you and your partner have kids together, this guideline still holds true. You only communicate with your ex-partner if it is absolutely required, according to this regulation. The interactions must be exclusively business-related and kept as brief as possible. Once the exchange is done, you resume your vow to avoid further contact.

- **The indefinite no contact rule:** As the name implies, this rule prohibits you from ever getting in touch with your former again. It's intriguing to observe that a lot of people begin with the traditional no-contact policy and then keep their distance since they don't want to restart their relationship with their former. As a result, they eventually progress to this form of the no-contact rule to move on. If you were in an abusive relationship, either physically or psychologically, you must abide by the indefinite no-contact rule. If your toxic former is a narcissist who wishes to micromanage every action you do, you must also adhere to this condition.

WHY IS THE NO CONTACT RULE SO SUCCESSFUL?

In order to recover, deal with, and regain power over your feelings, cutting contact enables you to construct your personal closure. It enables you to think through your emotions and finally choose how to move forward. When someone unfolds in front of you, you have the option to choose to fold according to the no-contact rule. It's a white flag in response to each of their red flags. The no-contact rule could also shatter your heart, regardless of whether you are enforcing it or on the receiving side of it. The "no contact rule" works so well because it shows acceptance of the relationship's end.

TIPS FOR GOING "NO CONTACT"

Going no contact is a self-preservation strategy that is suggested when it is necessary to detach yourself from a relationship due to a divorce, trauma bond rehabilitation, or toxic relationship. Going no contact is a technique that aids in heart healing without permanently impeding the healing of wounds brought on by engagement with another person. It helps in grieving loss and aids in ending a person's dependency.

- **Setting personal boundaries:** Keep your thoughts clear of your significant toxic one. Stop focusing on them, your relationships with them, how to resolve issues, your feelings toward them, etc. If you find yourself having daydreams about the things you wish were happening in your relationship, force yourself to stop and focus on anything that might be your hobby. No contact is more than just a physical practice. It also involves the mind.

- **Avoid all contact with your ex-partner:** The no-contact policy's initial step is to cease all communication. That entails refraining from contacting your ex via phone or text, social media, or by responding to their messages. Although severing ties with such a close person could be challenging, remember that this will help you move on.

- **Staying away from people who interact with this person:** Removing the toxic partner's friends from your social media accounts is another thing that is strongly advised to do in order to break off communication with them. Maybe you may have developed strong bonds with these individuals over the time of your relationship, but if you dated a narcissistic sociopath, she or he would probably plan a hate campaign about you, and you won't find any encouragement or support from them. Another possibility is if you're interacting with a buddy of your ex, your curiosity could get the better of you. A connection is being set up using this. Breaking all lines of communication is the goal of no contact. Avoid talking about the person; doing so makes it much simpler for you to adhere to the no-contact rule.

STICK WITH IT

The majority of those in toxic relationships are very reluctant to cut off communication. This is due to a variety of factors.

The key one is that unhealthy relationships have a propensity for addiction. The target's compulsion to "one day get it right" or mend it is the hook in a toxic relationship. Due to the obvious negative emotions it causes, such as guilt, duty, hope, desire, bewilderment, etc., the target continues to be trapped in the toxic relationship.

There are various strategies to make certain that you adhere to the contact strategy if it is difficult for you. Maintain your overall health by working out every day, sleeping on a normal schedule, practicing yoga to boost your immune system to become stronger and to help you to cope with stress, and participating in a daily meditation of your preference. Using all these meditations to help you be aware of your desires is a necessary component in the cycle of dependence on this toxic relationship. Understand that emotional manipulation and devaluation have actually "hooked" us to the narcissist by creating biochemical ties.

Most importantly, practice radical acceptance and attentiveness to the present time to have a positive connection with your desire to end no contact. Keep in mind that relapse could be an unavoidable aspect of the addictive cycle, and show kindness to yourself if you ever violate no contact.

You need to get back on the wagon after sliding off of it when you are practicing this self-compassion and forgiving. Keep a diary of your attempts to violate no contact to help you resist the impulse to act on it. Allow oneself at least thirty minutes to gather your thoughts before acting on any urges. It will gradually become simpler when you realize that violating no contact frequently results in only unpleasant learning opportunities rather than rewards.

If you really want to end your toxic relationship where your mental health degrades, you need closure. It cannot be given to you by the other person. Offer it to yourself first. Maintaining communication or conversations with your ex in an effort to reach some elusive "closure" is a failing strategy. Recognize that maintaining no contact is equivalent to quitting drinking or abusing drugs. It needs effort.

Similar to what a drug addict goes through when they quit using their preferred substance, you will go through detox and withdrawal phases. You have the chance to find strength inside yourself during the period following a toxic relationship and discover how to stand up for yourself.

CHAPTER 9
HOW TO HEAL THE BRAIN FROM RELATIONSHIP TRAUMA

Traumatic stress alters the chemical and structure of our brains, having a long-lasting effect on our behavior and how we see the world. Fortunately, with the right attention, its impact could gradually be reduced.
After going through a toxic relationship, they frequently show more stress in response to things and situations. Emotional trauma has been found to have a variety of effects on how the brain functions. The hippocampus, amygdala, and prefrontal cortex are the three parts of the brain primarily affected by the consequences of trauma. Each of these regions contributes to the control of emotions and the reaction to fear.

Those areas might behave and operate differently than they did before such emotional trauma. After an abusive relationship had ended due to the number of traumatic events that could take place in such a relationship. You might have symptoms of an acute stress reaction in the first month after a traumatic encounter. It affects your brain, and you might not be able to concentrate on your daily chores.

Before you heal your brain from relationship trauma, you need to understand how it affects the brain.

How Emotional Trauma Changes the Brain

The amygdala, hippocampus, and prefrontal cortex are the three sections of the brain that are most impacted by emotional trauma.

The brain's amygdala is a region of nerve tissue that controls feelings and impulses for survival and remembering. Fear detection is one of the amygdala's key functions. It detects dangers and gathers data about the surroundings around us. The amygdala detects threats through our senses, like sight and hearing, and responds by producing the emotion of fear. All of this occurs subconsciously, deep within our minds.

The amygdala is overactive when traumatized. People with emotional brain trauma frequently display greater dread of stressful stressors than most other people. When a stimulus is somehow related to the traumatic experience a person experienced, the amygdala could frequently become overactive. The brain's response to emotional trauma may result in long-term stress, heightened fear, and irritability. Additionally, it could be more difficult for people in pain to relax or even sleep as a result.

The limbic system of the brain includes the hippocampus.
It distinguishes between present and past events while primarily being in charge of preserving and retrieving memories. The hippocampus might experience physical effects as a result of trauma; studies have indicated that those with trauma may have a smaller hippocampus than average.

The hippocampus, which is primarily affected by trauma on the brain, will have an impact on trauma survivors' capacity to retain some memories. The survivors' minds may be plagued by other memories that are incredibly vivid. Environments that inadvertently trigger fear, stress, or panic in the trauma survivor may happen. This happens because the victim is unable to distinguish between the current circumstance and their recent experience. The brain then perceives a threat, triggering the fight-or-flight reaction.

The brain region that controls emotions is called the ventromedial prefrontal cortex. Following emotional trauma, this emotion-controlling region is frequently impacted and grows more sensitive to other brain regions. Normally, when the amygdala detects a negative feeling, such as fear, the prefrontal brain responds logically. However, following trauma, this rationalism might be suppressed, and your prefrontal brain will struggle to control emotions like terror.

Healing the Brain After Relationship Trauma

The good news is that it is possible to undo the brain changes that have occurred. The neurological system can recover to allow the amygdala to relearn to relax once again, the hippocampus to resume correct memory consolidation, and the flow between the responsive and restorative modes of the brain to resume.

Trauma healing is not something that can be accomplished quickly and easily. The process of recovering from trauma takes time, patience, and a lot of care. You must examine your background to determine how it all began. A therapist who is familiar with the intricacies of trauma reactions is required for this type of therapy. You can confront your emotional relationship with your abuser and move through your experience with the assistance of a therapist without feeling guilty or judged. There is no one "treatment" that can be used to treat trauma ties. Instead, numerous trauma-focused programs effectively help trauma survivors and can also be utilized to heal trauma ties.

The use of virtual reality, ketamine, and methylenedioxymethamphetamine (ecstasy), as well as medicines, hypnotherapy, neuro-linguistic programming, neurofeedback, cognitive therapy, as well as other brain-related modalities, is effective in treating PTSD. For the brain to reset itself, the mind must reinterpret and release the trauma.

- **Cognitive-behavioral therapy (CBT):** Using a conversation-based method like cognitive-behavioral therapy allows patients to examine problematic behavior patterns or painful memories. Finding new, better ways to manage stress could be facilitated by discussing these behaviors with a therapist.

- **Dialectical behavior therapy (DBT):** People who struggle with impulsive and emotional reactions can benefit from dialectical behavior therapy. Individuals might better understand their fears and anxieties and typical responses with the help of a therapist, then employ a variety of techniques to control their emotions healthily.

- **Somatic Therapy:** Treatment of trauma, mind, and body resets, and health restoration has all been successful through somatic experiences. A comprehensive therapy called somatic experiencing explores the interplay between both the mind and body in relationship to mental history. Somatic therapy aims to identify and relieve any tension in the body that may continue to be present in the body following trauma. The patient often keeps account of the emotions he or she feels throughout the body during counseling sessions. Somatic psychology therapy could involve moving or dancing while paying attention to your body's experiences, as well as breathing exercises, voice work, physical activity, and therapeutic touch.

- **Yoga therapy:** Since yoga therapy uses a body-based strategy to address the emotion held in the body by fostering mindfulness, consciousness, and inner calm, it might be a helpful addition to trauma treatment. A body-based method is more effective in releasing emotional difficulties as they frequently reside in the body's tissues. Firstly, you may master problems that are both physical and mental in the here-and-now and serenity of a position. The work also promotes the empowerment of the mind, body, and soul. Finally, individuals practice their new skills on the mat. After that, people use those skills in their daily lives so that they can live more completely in the present.

- **Pharmacotherapy:** It is the use of drugs to control and lessen the intensity of traumatic reactions. Although medications cannot make the pain go away, they may be used in conjunction with therapy to help you better process your trauma.

- **Exposure therapy:** Through continual exposure, exposure therapy, a type of behavior theory, attempts to lessen the dread of the traumatic experience. Exposure treatment has been demonstrated to promote social adjustment, lessen anxiety and depression, and organize traumatic memory.

- **EMDR Therapy:** Successful therapy for trauma, including post-traumatic stress disorder, is EMDR therapy (PTSD). Over 2 million individuals of all ages have reported feeling better because of EMDR. In addition to treating trauma, it is also beneficial for treating complicated grief, phobias, addictions, anxiety disorders, and other conditions. A person's brain undergoes some alterations as a result of the negative experience of a traumatic incident. Your brain's ability to digest information is harmed. The sensations associated with the trauma generally persist, and they can be brought up by current affairs. The brain's ability to process information is directly impacted by EMDR therapy, enabling the return of normal function.

Fortunately, doctors and mental health experts are becoming more conscious of the long-term effects of post-traumatic stress. People face trauma after being in toxic or abusive relationships. It can take time to heal from this toxic or abusive relationship.

Even while many patients in treatment continue to struggle with some aspects of post-traumatic anxiety throughout their lives, receiving the right care could help patients develop coping skills and get a better understanding of and ability to control their mental health. Getting assistance is not a sign of shame. Always get assistance from a mental health or medical expert when you or a close one are worried about handling a traumatic event (or sequence of events) that you've gone through. Your ability to operate and be happy daily depends on your mental health. It's crucial to be kind and sympathetic to yourself while you make the decision. Dealing with the trauma's related thoughts, emotions, and responses could be necessary for recovery. Recovery takes time, assistance, and processing at a speed that is comfortable for you.

CHAPTER 10
HOW TO STOP A NARCISSISTIC ABUSE CYCLE

It is much more painful to be in a narcissistic relationship than to wonder what a happy marriage sounds like. You are consumed by it from the inside out to the point where you don't even recognize yourself. A cycle of narcissistic abuse must be broken to break the emotions of guilt, humiliation, fury, and misery that it causes. Behavior that is narcissistic or entitled is harmful. The cycle of narcissistic abuse may continue for many years, months, or even a lifetime. Numerous narcissists associate with codependents who satisfy their need for adoration. Furthermore, it might be challenging to recognize that you are being gaslighted if you have never had professional guidance.

You are reduced to levels no human should always experience, which dehumanizes you. Nevertheless, you may learn how to liberate yourself and stop the narcissistic abuse cycle. Recovering from narcissistic abuse is doable, and there is a possibility.

What Is the Narcissistic Cycle of Abuse?

The abusive pattern of behavior that defines the relationships of individuals with narcissistic features is known as the "narcissistic abuse cycle." It entails idealizing someone at first, depreciating them afterward, and continuing the cycle until they are ultimately discarded after they are no longer useful. The three stages of the narcissistic cycle of abuse:

- **Idealization:** Everyone who has ever been in a romantic affair will be able to remember those early emotions of delight and satisfaction they experience when they first meet someone. For example, when you initially started dating your lover, did you experience euphoria? This occurs frequently. There's a good reason why this phase of a relationship is called the honeymoon stage. This narcissistic abuse cycle, however, takes things to an entirely new level. The narcissist would elevate and idealize their new partner. This goes beyond merely believing they have discovered the "correct" person. Instead, they give their new partner their whole attention because they believe they have discovered perfection.

- **Devaluation:** Whenever the honeymoon phase fades out for the majority of couples, things start to settle into a regular manner or habit. You are still capable of loving your lover deeply. That initial high, though, usually passes. However, this is the stage when the majority of couples begin to develop deeper bonds and teach one another how to function as a team. This stage of the relationship is very different, though, in the narcissistic abuse cycle. It's when, rather than getting closer to their lover, the narcissist starts to undervalue them. They acknowledge that their partner isn't ideal (and besides, who is?), and therefore they no longer value them. One's perception of their very own importance and self-worth is the only thing that gives them value. As a result, the narcissist starts to blame their partner or refrain from having intimate or affectionate moments. The narcissist may turn the situation around and accuse their partner whenever their partner pushes, which gives them more room that will further devalue them.

- **Rejection:** Successful relationships typically progress to the stage when they do not just get along but also thrive together. This may have happened to other couples or perhaps to you personally. Partners can finish each other's words, understand one another's thoughts, and just "connect." They disagree and sometimes even fight from time to time, of course. They can still talk to one another and work out their differences. On the other hand, a narcissist starts to distance themselves from their spouse and eventually dumps them in favor of a new partnership that meets their desires.

The sequence of downs and ups or cycles of hope and terror characterizes the cycle of narcissistic abuse. A narcissist will manipulate you, make grand gestures, and gaslight you to mislead and hurt you. The impulse to leave and the obligation to remain will conflict with one another.

How to Stop the Cycle of Abuse

It is frustrating to experience a narcissist's abusive cycle. It starts with a distressing occurrence. The narcissist then retaliates violently after getting attacked. The victim, weary of the assault, dependably fights back. As more proof that they are being abused, the narcissist defends their abusive behavior. When the abused collapses or surrenders, the narcissist feels validated, and the cycle repeats.

- **Understand that you're being abused:** Attacking their victims, telling them they're overly sensitive, that they won't ever find someone who will treat them differently, and emotionally manipulating them into thinking the abuse never occurred are all techniques used by narcissists. You should record abusive behaviors, so you don't recall them or believe something different happened. You can begin the journey out of this relationship when you realize that all the emotional blackmail and immediate emotional connection is only a pretext for the depreciation and rejection stages down the road.

- **Embrace self-compassion:** Understanding how to recover after narcissistic abuse in a relationship can be aided by exercising self-compassion. You might discover that blaming yourself is what comes to mind first. It could require some time for you to cease judging the actions that helped to build the relationship. Assure yourself that it is not your responsibility if anyone treats you poorly. Appreciate yourself for eventually reaching a point that allows you to recover and leave the situation.

- **System of Support:** The significance of a support system was already mentioned. Let's be clear: doing this all by yourself would make things considerably more challenging. You must therefore seek the advice of reliable sources. Yes, I am aware that you most likely disregarded them while the two of you were still together. You even severed relations with the majority of your relatives and didn't answer your closest friend's messages. Nevertheless, these are your folks. They completely comprehend all you were suffering through, and I'm able to assure you that they will embrace you with arms wide open. Take the initiative, then, and contact them. Inform them you want to leave and seek their help.

- **Set boundaries:** Boundaries are guidelines for how you should be handled. People would treat you in the manner that you permit. To express your boundaries, you must be aware of them. This entails becoming aware of your emotions, paying attention to your body, being aware of your rights, and developing assertiveness. They have to be clear. Don't leave clues or assume others are mind readers. Nevertheless, failing to establish limits might leave you feeling resentful, uncomfortable, and unsupported. You have a right to these boundaries; therefore, it's crucial that you give them some thought. The following are a few instances of boundaries:

    1. Refusing to put up with any teasing.
    2. Avoid providing them with cash or any other form of financial support.
    3. Leaving if the narcissist becomes aggressive.
    4. Limit the amount of time you spend together.

- **Don't accept promises, demand action:** Narcissists are excellent at predicting their future behavior. Sadly, they don't always carry through. Demanding rapid change is a necessity if you choose to keep a relationship with a narcissist but want the abuse cycle to end. Set clear expectations for what they should accomplish if you would like to keep this relationship going.

- **Be Patient:** Even successful relationships might occasionally be challenging. Things could be much more difficult when you're trying to heal from a relationship that involves narcissistic abuse. Remain patient with the process of healing as well as with yourself. You'll discover that as time passes, you can begin to let go of the relationship and go on. You'll eventually conclude that you merit having wholesome connections in your life. The secret to your healing is patience.

- **Walk away unannounced:** There is no way a confrontation with your abuser will go well. They might get angry, but they will probably try to drag you deeper into the pattern. The narcissist may express regret, promise to make changes, and then return to their old behavior a day or two later. Many victims of narcissistic abuse would make an effort to make things work, and with the right expectations and boundaries, the narcissist might even transform. However, since it won't satisfy their demands, the majority of narcissists won't want to remain in a relationship with all these limitations. In that situation, leaving rather than engaging in more abuse is preferable for both parties.

- **Step up your defenses:** Whenever upset, narcissists fight violently. Therefore, you should enter the situation with that expectation. They might launch a smear campaign to turn your loved ones and even employees against you. Narcissists are constantly attempting to win over people, but if you're ready for the campaign, you could fight back.

Narcissists leave behind wounds that prevent their victims from leading regular lives. They upset the victim's mind in addition to causing them emotional harm. Every feeling of self-worth or self-love is lost by the sufferer. Thus, it is crucial ito break the pattern of abuse. I hope that the aforementioned ideas will help you in breaking the cycle.

CHAPTER 11
SET BOUNDARIES WITH TOXIC PEOPLE

In this chapter, we will talk about the various ways through which you can set boundaries with your toxic partner. Setting boundaries with toxic people is not an easy task, but it is something achievable. Setting up boundaries from toxic people is a must to protect your peace of mind and save your energy, and when you succeed at this, you feel empowered.

Toxic people can be ruthless in a way that they do not respect your needs and constantly violate your personal space, making it necessary for you to effectively communicate your boundaries to them. Setting boundaries is also a way of telling your partner what they can expect from you and how you want to be treated.

IDENTIFY AND LIVE BY YOUR CORE VALUES

We are all guided by our moral compass; sometimes, all we need is a little help recognizing them. You need to recognize the fundamental beliefs that serve as your guiding principle. Once you identify your guiding principles, your moral compass will tell you what are the things or behaviors that you can not or must not tolerate.

This is a clarity that sometimes most people in a toxic relationship lack, and they let their partners treat them in any way their partner feels right. Therefore you must have clarity on what are the behaviors that are not acceptable or tolerable by you. This is the first and one of the most important steps towards empowering yourself against your toxic partner and will help you set up your boundaries right.

HAVE PATIENCE AND COMMUNICATE YOUR BOUNDARIES EFFECTIVELY

Having recognized what behaviors are acceptable and what behaviors are not from your partner towards you, you now need to communicate it to your partner. There are a few things that you might need to keep in mind while communicating your boundaries to your partner to avoid tension during the conversation:

- Assert your requirements and offsets to them in a calm and clear manner
- Do not put any blame on them during the conversation
- Express your boundaries in simple and crisp terms without over-explaining things. The moment you start to explain your needs, your words start losing their value.
- Remember you are expressing your needs, so focus on what you want to say without thinking of how you feel when they disrespect your boundaries.

When you are in a relationship with a toxic person, they can trigger you at any point in time. Thus, always take a deep breath before communicating anything, even before communicating your boundaries.

REMIND YOURSELF THEIR BEHAVIOR IS THEIR STUFF, NOT YOURS

If your partner is making you feel uncomfortable and drained, then it is not okay. Even after you have successfully communicated your boundaries to your partner, their nature may cause them to behave or say hurtful things. Disrespecting someone's boundaries is completely their stuff and has nothing to do with you. Even if you had thought or your partner made you believe that this was your mistake or you could not communicate the boundary properly, do not fall into that trap.

BEFORE REACTING, PAUSE FOR A MOMENT

You will reset the boundary the moment you give a loud reaction to your partner. Your toxic partner might have been looking for such a reaction, and by reacting the way they want, you are shifting from your core values, erasing the boundary, and giving power to your partner's hand. To avoid this, you need to pause before you respond to any of your partner's comments or questions. It is natural for humans to give a loud and negative reaction without thinking it through much. Therefore, the next time you are in a similar situation, count to ten in your head before responding. You can also ask yourself questions like:

- Is this more important than my mental peace?

- Two days or weeks down the line, will it be this important?

And other relevant questions to help you decide whether or not to respond to their snide behavior.

START USING THE WORD "NO"

"No" is a single word that is extremely powerful in setting boundaries against not just your partner but any toxic person. You need to start saying no to things that make you uncomfortable or upset. More often than not, individuals tolerate or do uncomfortable things for their partner because they feel guilty otherwise. Being in a relationship does not mean that you have to be a people pleaser. You need not make their choices or decisions a priority at all times. Your mental health and well-being are equally important.

The next time you are asked to do something or behave in a way that does not feel right to you, say no. Do not feel guilty or listen to anyone trying to make you feel bad about it, as you have all the right to refuse things that do not feel right to you.

VISUALIZE A BUBBLE PROTECTING YOU

This may seem a little insane, but visualize that you are always surrounded by a protective bubble, protecting you from negative energy. This is a very useful way to set boundaries as you are using your mind to protect yourself from negative energy. Your mind is one of the strongest pieces of equipment to protect yourself from all the toxic behaviors from your partner. How does it work?

Every day when you wake up, meditate for two minutes and convince yourself that you are surrounded by a protective bubble at all times. You can tell yourself small positive affirmations like:

- Only positive things will enter the bubble today.
- Only love can reach me today inside the bubble

Or any other affirmation that is fit for your situation.

START PRACTICING DETACHMENT

Detachment is a healthy shift from a chaotic situation. In a relationship, suppose your partner accuses you of something untrue or does something that acts as your trigger; no matter how calm you are, chances are you try to control the situation or explain to them what is right. This is how you are not keeping a boundary by over-explaining things or getting yourself into a conversation that holds no value. To set boundaries, you need to start practicing detachment from your partner or certain disturbing situations. Some of the things that you can do to practice detachment from your toxic partner are:

- By responding to the situation in a way that you normally would not. For example, instead of justifying something, tell them it is not right and close the chapter.
- Leaving the situation or the conversation. You may find this rude or against your morals, but when it is to protect your sanity, you have to leave the situation, and it is not rude.
- Limit the amount of time you are spending with your partner to escape their manipulation.

- Choose not to indulge in conversations or arguments that have already happened once and did not take a good shape or form or were resolved.

CUT DOWN THE TIME YOU SPEND WITH THEM

Again, if someone is adversely affecting your mental peace, the best thing you can do is cut down the time you spend with them. Some relationships start well and get toxic eventually. You do not want to avoid them, but cutting down on the time you spend with them will give both of you ample time to reflect on things.

In the worst situations, to keep your boundaries, you may also cut them out of your life. You might be ignoring the bad behaviors or bad side of your partner for family's sake, but that is never the solution. Talk to them and tell them why you feel you need to end the relationship. You must never put anything above your overall well-being. If it means cutting down on the time you spend with your partner or simply moving on from the relationship, do it without looking back.

TELL YOUR PARTNER THE THINGS THAT YOU ARE NOT AVAILABLE FOR

It is always a good way to set boundaries by explicitly telling your partner about the things that you cannot be emotionally or physically available for. If your partner is constantly telling you that you are a bad parent, remind them that it is not right and that you will not tolerate remarks like this. Communication is the key, even in a toxic relationship. Thus, make sure you are communicating, sometimes even over-communicating things that you are not available for.

Setting boundaries against your partner by limiting contact or putting yourself and your needs first is a very important step towards empowering yourself and moving on from a toxic relationship.

CHAPTER 12
REBUILD SELF-ESTEEM AFTER GETTING OUT OF A TOXIC RELATIONSHIP

The number of toxic relationships in this world is more than we can ever expect, and it breaks my heart when individuals go back to their partners after a break-up simply because their self-esteem is low. After break up, it is natural for you to feel different as regardless of the reason for the split, it is always difficult. You might end up blaming yourself if you overthink, as it affects your self-esteem. The best way to cope with post-break-up grief and to prevent yourself from becoming miserable is by rebuilding your self-esteem after getting out of the toxic relationship; even your boundaries will fall apart.

BEGIN THE JOURNEY TOWARDS EMOTIONAL HEALING

Moving out of a toxic relationship helps you to understand what you want and do not want in a relationship, and thus now is the best time to channel all the energy toward building yourself as a better person. Start your journey towards emotional healing, and it will automatically boost your self-esteem. You can start this journey with simple steps like journaling. When you keep things within yourself, you start to suffocate and get caged with negative thoughts. These negative thoughts must be let out to get back the confidence and rebuild your self-esteem.

Journaling for 10-15 minutes or even 5 minutes daily at the beginning or end of your day helps a lot. Write all the emotions that you feel within yourself, and let it all out. Speak about the good parts as well as the bad parts in the relationship, discuss with yourself why it went stale, and you will identify that whatever happened was due to the toxicity of your partner, or if you are the toxic person, then you will recognize that as well.

This recognition will help you get a clearer picture of the situation and bring you peace. You will also realize how strong you are to have been able to get out of the relationship.

PRACTICE SELF LOVE AND SELF CARE

Post break up, most individuals are quick to get themselves immersed in work to keep themselves busy. While it is important to keep the mind busy, and I will discuss this in a later section, it is equally important to love yourself a little bit more and care for yourself. Remember when you were young, and you had a bad day, your parents or best friend would give you a hug or a treat, was it not that comforting? It was because they were showering their love on you. Now that you are an adult or a teenager, you need to do that for yourself.

In a toxic relationship, the one thing that you lost was self-love, making it extremely important to care for yourself a little bit more after getting out of the relationship. There is no hard and fast rule that you have to indulge yourself in some extravagance or go on a vacation like people advise you to, to pamper yourself. Doing simple things like taking a hot shower, re-watching your favorite movie, sleeping for an extra hour, doing your hair, wearing makeup, or simply wearing your favorite bow tie can help. If you have a pet, give them a warm hug or stand in front of the mirror and tell yourself, "I love myself!" Work on your self-relationship, love yourself the way you would want to be loved, care for yourself, and make yourself your absolute favorite and you will no longer need to worry about re-building your self-esteem.

COME TO TERMS WITH YOUR FEELINGS

Are you feeling low? Are you feeling upset? Do you want to cry? Are you angry?
Ask yourself questions like these and identify how you feel instead of trying to suppress them. There is no point showing a bold face outside without facing your inner storm first.

Self-esteem is something that you can build or break from within. Come to terms with how you feel, good or bad. Acknowledge the emotion and heal from it. Unless and until you are true to your feelings, your self-esteem can not be rebuilt. Let me assure you, my dear reader, that no person feels happy right after they move out of a toxic relationship. Yes, you may feel relieved, but it is okay to be a little upset. Do not blame yourself for how you feel; instead, acknowledge the feeling and heal.

Another aspect of a post-breakup is when you feel hatred and anger towards your partner for damaging you. They have already done a lot to mess things up for you; you do need to pet these negative emotions as they will only harm you and your well-being. Hating your toxic partner or yourself does not help in rebuilding your self-esteem. Let these emotions go.

DEVELOP POSITIVE HABITS

I have heard my readers tell me that after a breakup, their partner's friends chime in with their negativity. Or sometimes, the person picks up bad habits to cope with the situation, do not do that! Instead, develop positive habits like fighting the urge to take everything to heart, returning to your values, and so on. When you listen to others and take each negative word to your heart, you become more vulnerable. Instead, return to your core values as they will help you to put a filter on what to listen to and what things need to be filtered out.

Cleaning is another positive habit that helps to get back your self-confidence. Turn on the music, clean your house or room, and declutter things, it will help you clear your mind. A clear mind helps you stay positive and does not hamper your self-esteem.

IMBIBE YOURSELF IN THINGS THAT MAKE YOU HAPPY

When you are in a relationship with a toxic person, you lose your energy and sometimes forget to do things that make you happy. After a breakup, start doing everything that makes you truly happy and try out everything that you want to.
Immerse yourself in your favorite book for hours, learn guitar, eat popcorn, and watch your favorite soccer game on the big screen - do everything you want to. Do the things you wanted to do but could not, as your partner claimed it to be annoying, and free yourself from their voice.

Most importantly, respect yourself. Respecting ourselves is the key to strong self-esteem. Toxic relationships sometimes shake things up and make your identity slightly blurry. Start respecting yourself again and regain your true self back.

BE GRATEFUL TO YOURSELF

Remember, it is difficult to get away from a toxic partner, yet you have made it. You identified their patterns and chose to walk away from them. It takes a lot of courage and strength to do it. Be grateful to yourself for being so strong and for standing up for yourself. When you start seeing how much it took from you to get out of the toxic place, you will realize how strong you are. You will be grateful to yourself, and that is empowering.

The moment you start seeing your strengths, your self-confidence, and your self-esteem will automatically be regained. Start reminding yourself of your amazing qualities, your strength, and your incredible journey toward freedom. Never forget about your positive qualities and traits or let anybody tell you otherwise.

FIND YOURSELF A SUPPORT SYSTEM

You are worthy of a beautiful life, and when you are constantly reminded of this, your self-esteem is automatically boosted. You have to remember that there is more in your beautiful life than the toxic love from a toxic partner. Find yourself a support system to constantly remind you of this. It can be work besties or college friends but make sure you are staying connected to your trusted friends. In times like this, when your self-esteem is low, the words of your supportive friend help as a boost; thus, staying close to them helps.

You can also find a support system online or in your family. Your parents or elder siblings have also gone through their heartbreaks and are a little wiser than you are at present.

Anyone who is helping you rebuild your self-esteem, take their hand instead of shutting them out.

I know that sometimes there are sudden lows after a breakup, and that may cause you to feel you are going nowhere, but that is not true. Do not stick to the feeling of low; instead, constantly remind yourself of how much you have grown after a breakup.

The story of your life will not always be all rainbows and bursts of sunshine; sometimes, it will be gloomy and stormy that does not mean it will be permanent. Work on rebuilding your self-esteem, and do not let it shatter again.

CHAPTER 13

TOXIC RELATIONSHIPS AND THEIR FORMS

As discussed in previous chapters, a toxic relationship is detrimental to your health, mental health, and overall well-being. Yet some of us stay trapped in it for a long time before finally realizing the truth. Why does it happen?

Simple, toxic relationships come in different forms, just like different hues of a particular color. Thus, identifying them becomes difficult at times. In this chapter, I will talk about all the different forms of toxic relationships so that next time you can recognize the signs and take necessary measures before it starts affecting you.

THE DICTATOR RELATIONSHIP

Have you watched the movie *The Dictator*? The concept is there is a dictator who wants to control everything around him, even the lives of his people. Some partners are like that. They want to control everything in the relationship, including you.

It is natural for partners to ask their partner to refrain from doing some things that they do not like or saying things that are against their core values, but when a partner starts nagging you with everything, then there is a problem. A controlling partner wants to approve or disapprove of what you wear (every time); they constantly want to know where you are and what you are doing, even if that means disrupting your work.

You have no say in anything in the relationship; it is always about them - what they like, what they want to do, and how they want to do things. If you feel that your life is getting controlled or micro-managed, then you are definitely in a toxic relationship with a dictator.

THE OVER-RELIANT RELATIONSHIP

The over-reliant partner is someone who wants all their decisions to be made by you. Initially, you might find it cute that your partner is asking your opening in everything out of love and respect, but one wrong decision and you are in a spot. The over-reliant or over-dependent partners have their anxiety and fear of decision-making due to the negative consequences of a wrong decision and thus want you to decide for them.

As long as the outcomes of your decisions are in their favor, everything goes fine, but as soon as something goes wrong, they get passive-aggressive with you. For example, you are going on a dinner date, and they ask you to pick the restaurant. Now, if they do not enjoy the night or the food, they have someone to put all the blame on.

Now, they will ridicule you for choosing the restaurant or keep reminding you of your bad decision. In extreme cases, they behave passively aggressively to the extent that your mind and energy get drained, and you are constantly exhausted. This kind of toxic relationship is not easy to identify, and the result is you are constantly anxious as you are scared that they will again behave in a way that will agitate you. Nobody deserves to live in constant fear of making a wrong decision, especially in a romantic relationship. In extreme cases, it will shatter your self-confidence and make you doubt all your life choices, making you a gullible person.

THE PUPPET MASTER RELATIONSHIP

The puppet master is the partner who is constantly playing games with you. They will be very sweet, understanding, and supportive of you most of the time, which camouflages their true intentions. You can also call them the users, as they only want more and more from you, and for that, they twist their words and constantly try to manipulate you. You do not want to be with someone whose only requirement is that things should always go their way. Such partners do not have the guts to say things upfront to your face and are constantly playing with words. Such relationships are exhausting as you no longer have clarity on what is happening or why it is happening. The worst part is the manipulator will make you believe that you are never doing enough for them, like the way they are doing for you.

THE INSECURE PARTNER

We meet a lot of people in our daily lives, especially if our job demands so. A little insecurity in a relationship is understandable, but if your partner is someone who is constantly doubting you, scared they will lose you, or needs constant assurance that you still love them, then it is a toxic relationship. A relationship should be a safe space where both partners can share their thoughts and opinions, not a courtroom where you constantly need to prove your love and loyalty to them. If your partner is showing signs of constant insecurity, then it is time for you to sit with them and tell them that the relationship is getting toxic. If possible, you can try and understand why they are being so insecure all the time, but if nothing helps, you need to take a call. Insecurity is often the result of being treated badly in the past or from personal experiences; however, you should not suffer due to your partner's emotional baggage.

THE GASLIGHTER

A gaslighter is a person who always criticizes you for everything you do and makes you doubt your self-worth. In such relationships, your partner will blame you for everything happening with you, with them, and around you. Their statements always start and end with "I told you so." This kind of relationship is extremely harmful as they not only make you self-doubt but make you feel guilty for things you have not done. They make you feel guilty for doing or not doing the simplest of things. For example, you told them you would call them in 5 minutes, but due to some work, you forgot. They will point it out to you and play the victim and make you feel guilty for being a bad partner.

From time to time, they will also work towards lifting the guilt feeling from you to make you feel better. By doing this, they are holding power over you and are constantly controlling you.
A gaslighter is also the kind of person who might make you feel as if you were nothing before you met them and belittle you on every other occasion and are one of the most toxic kinds of people to exist.
If you notice these signs in your relationship, then you need to get out of it at the earliest as these kinds of partners are never at fault. They will destroy your self-esteem and take the joy out of your life.

RELATIONSHIP WITH THE TOP PERFECTIONIST

It may feel great to be in a relationship with a perfectionist, but the moment they become a top perfectionist, bad things start happening. A perfectionist will want everything to be done in the best possible way, and every time that does not happen, they lose their stability. They start scolding you or creating an unnecessary scene. A top perfectionist will also constantly find faults in you, from the way you do things to the way you conduct yourself. Do you want to be in a relationship with someone who constantly finds your faults? No, right. There is a healthy relationship where your partner will help you fill in the holes, but with a top perfectionist, you are just constantly under scrutiny.

THE ABUSIVE RELATIONSHIP

When I say abusive relationship, I am not talking about physical abuse only. Abusive relationships also include verbal abuse. If your partner ever raises a hand on you, that should be the end of your relationship. If somebody truly loves you, they will make mistakes, as it is inevitable but never the mistake of raising their hand to you.
Another classic example of a toxic relationship is trying to control their partner through intimidation. If your partner is threatening you or intimidating you, you then know it is a toxic relationship. Using words to make you cry on purpose or to make you feel terrible is verbal abuse.

You should never tolerate your partner saying ill things to you, as if you do that once, they will become more dominant and keep repeating this behavior. They will later come and say sorry and try to fix things. This cycle marks a toxic, abusive relationship.

Always remember that some people may not be bad people, but their personalities contribute to the toxicity of the relationship. This chapter should help you to identify if you are in a toxic relationship when you feel something is wrong, but you are confused. Your partner might have been loving initially, but gradually they start to behave differently and start exhausting you. The chapter should be able to clear your doubt on whether you guys are simply incompatible or if your partner and the relationship are truly toxic.

CHAPTER 14

MOVING ON AFTER A TOXIC RELATIONSHIP

Initially, it may seem almost impossible to move on after you have been in a toxic relationship but remember, if there is a will, there is a way. Toxic relationships can be addictive and sometimes haunting, besides being astonishingly hurting and destructive. Addiction to your partner is the consequence of a toxic relationship. Another consequence is an emotional dependency on your partner, and after a breakup, individuals may end up having anxiety and depression besides low self-esteem and insecurities. You must move on and live the happier and healthier life that you deserve. The points discussed below are curated after consulting with relationship counselors and psychologists and will help you move on gracefully after a toxic relationship.

ACCEPTANCE OF THE REALITY

According to psychologists, breaking up a relationship causes grief which is equivalent to bereavement grief. Whether the relationship was toxic or not, you ought to feel the grief that will lead you to look back at the good days in the relationship. You may also see your partner through rose-colored glasses and try to justify the actions and look for other complex and non-existent reasons that might have caused the breakup.

This is a vicious trait that can be overcome only by accepting reality for what it is. Your partner was toxic, and you had to get out of it for your good, period. If you want to move on, then this is the first and most crucial step that you must adhere to. Having accepted the reality, you will be hit with a wave of emotions - it can be anger, sadness, or a mix of it all.

It is okay to feel these emotions. Sometimes hiding or brushing off the true emotions may seem like the easier thing to do, but it is a temporary and weak solution. Coming to terms with your true emotions and making certain adjustments in your life to overcome them is what will truly help you move on faster from the toxic relationship.

STOP TRYING TO GET A CLOSURE

When you are hurt by the person with whom you are deeply and truly in love, you often tend to not understand why they did what they did. You might want to wait around for them to apologize and get closure. Sorry to burst the bubble, but that apology or closure is almost never going to come.

You can not expect a person who caused you so much pain to explain things to you. You need to be the bigger and wiser person here and accept that moving on from the relationship is the best decision that you could have taken for yourself.

Waiting for their apology or closure will push you to the path of self-destruction. Your partner, with his/her toxic nature, has done enough harm to you already. You need not follow their path and destroy your life further. You did not deserve the atrocious treatment, whatever their reason may have been, and thus do not wait for their statement.

BE KIND TO YOURSELF

Some romantic partners can be toxic to the point that they make you lose your personality. They cage you in the toxic relationship in such a way that there is no chance for your growth and development, and you are afraid to speak your mind. You have already done a terrific job by moving out of the toxic environment, and now it is time for you to move on. In this phase, you must remember that change does not happen in a single day. It is a gradual process, and you can not expect yourself to be happy again in a single day. Be kind to yourself for feeling gloomy on most days.

Do not be a sufferer of the treatment you have been facing but at the same time, be a little kinder to yourself. Allow yourself time to heal and gain your true self back. You have just stepped out of a toxic relationship, be grateful to yourself for making it happen instead of beginning a toxic relationship with yourself.

RECOGNIZE THAT YOU ARE WORTHY OF HEALTHY LOVE

Part of your problem might be you have grown up with single parents or non-loving parents or have insecurities that make you feel you are not worthy of healthy love. Regardless of who you are, what you do, what color you are, or what shape you are - you deserve a healthy and loving relationship that helps you to grow. There is a famous quote that says, "we accept the love that we feel we deserve," and it is true. Until the time you realize that you deserve a healthy relationship where your partner will be loving and supportive, you will keep attracting toxic partners.

If it is difficult for you to believe that, and sometimes it may be difficult after moving out of a toxic relationship, then you must seek the help of those who are positive people. Spend time with your friends or family members who love you and are not toxic. It will help you recognize the true meaning of being loved. Loving and being loved are different; you need to feel healthy love, and that will help you understand that you deserve nothing less than a healthy relationship.

DO NOT TRY TO FILL THE VOID WITH ANOTHER RELATIONSHIP

After a toxic relationship ends, there appears a huge void in their place. You may want to fill the void but do not do so by jumping into a rebound relationship. It is important to take your time to heal after a painful breakup. The time being single is the best time to introspect things better and analyze things. Go back to meet your friends and family members often. This will help you move on from the toxic relationship while ensuring the void in your life is also getting filled.

In case you feel desperate or frustrated, then share it with those whom you can trust. Friends and families are always a safe outlet for all your emotions, and thus confide in them instead of jumping into another relationship which will lead you to an unknown territory again.

RECOGNIZE THE PERKS OF THE BREAKUP

As mentioned in one of the previous sections, it is human nature to look back at the relationship with rose-colored glasses. Instead, do a different exercise where you need to look at the post-breakup perks. You will be surprised at what comes out of the exercise. You may realize that the perk of the break up is:

- Now you have the freedom to express yourself better without the fear of being judged, going unheard, or insulted.

- You may now have the chance to pursue or do things that you want to do

- You may have the freedom not to do certain things that you were forced to do while in a toxic relationship.

There will be occasions when you still end up thinking of the perks of the relationship. Counter the thoughts by identifying if it is something non-negotiable. For example, the perk of the relationship may have been having a home to live in, but does that mean you cannot have a home being single? Crash at your friend's place or siblings' house temporarily till you find your place.

GIVE YOURSELF A TREAT

Motivate yourself to stay on the path of moving on from the relationship by treating yourself. There is a difference between a treat and an escapism. Treating yourself means reading your favorite book and getting immersed in it completely before going to bed or continuing with your daily work.

Escapism means reading the book throughout the day without facing the real world. Escapism can be melancholic, and you do not want to do that, but you must celebrate little victories in your battle toward moving on from a toxic relationship.

Your biggest victory is to have stepped out of the toxic relationship.

PRACTICE SPEAKING POSITIVE AFFIRMATIONS TO YOURSELF

Positive affirmations are extremely powerful in bringing about changes and reaching your goals. Speaking positive affirmations to yourself will only make you stronger and help you stay on track. Start telling yourself that you are strong, and you will eventually feel empowered. Similarly, you can accept the fact that you deserve a healthy and beautiful relationship by repeating sentences like, "I deserve a healthy relationship" every day to yourself. Affirmations are making yourself believe that you can achieve it and that you can move on from the toxic relationship.

Moving on after a toxic relationship can feel overwhelming, but you need to stay strong. Remember, this is one last battle toward closing this chapter of the past. Thus stay strong, and you will eventually move on gracefully.

CHAPTER 15
REALITY OF HEALING

Even when you're deeply in love, your relationship is toxic. Simply said, it can't go on. You lie all night long rehearsing the battles in your mind. You struggle to comprehend why your partner won't act differently or how they manage to blatantly disregard your feelings. Do they still genuinely love you? You ponder. Everything else you've done to try to just save your relationship has worked. Though the idea of ending it and being alone terrifies you, you realize the moment has come.

In our world, there are some things that can harm us so severely that we fail to see the damage. The effects of the after could no longer be relied upon, and the things you were unaware of become inevitable. Until you are unable to do anything at all, spending the majority of the day wallowing in your tears and doubting whether you will ever comprehend what it feels like to be whole and healthy once more.
Maybe you're simply too damaged to be repaired. However, the discomfort is now too great to bear. You could entirely lose yourself if you don't put an end to this right away. Sometimes you have to enter healing expecting to be broken where we've repaired improperly and recklessly and bruised more severely than the thing that injured you. So, when you finally decide to break the ties and start the healing process, you can face many difficulties.

The Painful Truth of Overcoming a Toxic Relationship

Relationships are essential to human existence, and despite our reluctance to acknowledge them, we rely on them. You may be sure that every person you know has a weakness for the individuals in their lives. A toxic relationship could cause a wide range of issues in our lives, much like improper medicine could hurt our bodies.

It drains you to experience the ups and downs of adoring and losing someone toxic to you. You are left there fully exposed and unable to breathe as it drains your life from you and scares you to your very core. You are left without anything. You feel bewildered, perplexed, and unsure of what you might have done wrong to receive this. You feel resentful that you could have been so inadequate to tolerate such things for such a prolonged period.

It's not a simple road. It takes much more time to recover than from a typical breakup. One of the most difficult things to accept is that. How come you can't let go of the individual who didn't even treat you properly and put them away from your mind? It's annoying. Some mornings are going to be difficult for you to get out of bed. It strikes you just as you start to think like you are recovering once more. It pulls the cover off, leaving you trembling and attempting to regain control of your emotions and sanity. You are left feeling numb and chilly, wondering how you arrived here and whether there is a way to return to where you came from.

You have gone through a terrifying experience that has altered you. You were crushed and made to experience suffering. You started to struggle and must now re-learn how to live. The connection was toxic. Not only were you, but so were the people you dated. You kept allowing people to hurt you repeatedly. You gave them back each time they damaged you. You gave them one more opportunity. Like you were enjoying the discomfort. However, you didn't. You simply had an addiction. People are addicted, just like all harmful things are.

There is a gap that has to be filled since a piece is absent. So, you temporarily fill it with other bad habits. Many more toxic people can start to attract you. But everything is a part of the learning process. All of it is necessary for healing. For so long, toxicity has been all you have known. Fighting, splitting apart, and then repeating the cycle has been your existence. You don't even understand the fundamental elements of a healthy relationship.

You don't know where to look for it. But as time passes, you become aware of it. Realizing that your relationship with this person was flawed. You realize that a good relationship doesn't involve screaming, arguing, and stomping out the door, regardless of how much love and happiness existed there. Lack of consistency, maybes, and sleepless evenings spent waiting for answers are not signs of a healthy partnership.

WHY IS IT SO DIFFICULT TO OVERCOME

Healing calls for you to accept how you have been handled in the relationship, which is among the factors that can make leaving a toxic relationship so challenging. So many traumatized people get locked in this situation. Change necessitates calming the nervous system as well as letting go of the person who was formerly vital to survival. This makes mending seem uncertain and even harmful. Your cognitive brain might well be mostly "offline" if you are caught in survival mode as a result of ongoing stress and trauma. The bottom regions of your brain, which are in charge of maintaining you alive and linked in the present, are where you are functioning.

Secondly, healing carries risks and doesn't guarantee a better quality of life. It might even seem like extra labor. It is necessary for change that we accept the threat has gone so that our cognitive brain can start engaging and reorganizing, and the stress response system may be turned off. It demands that we let go of abilities that are no more adaptable but rather dysfunctional, making us exposed and unpleasant. It necessitates that we acquire new abilities, alter our perspective, and adjust our boundaries.

Thirdly, "Why did I allow this to happen?" It is a common question we hear from people who are healing from previous relationships. Why am I not well? It can be difficult to ask these questions of yourself while being polite, compassionate, and curious. Learning how to softly and kindly question oneself is a fantastic first step toward mending your connection with yourself, as opposed to using these questions as a way of placing blame on yourself.

It's much simpler to see all the warning indications of a toxic relationship when the relationship has ended than it is to do so while it is still going on. To avoid spiraling into self-doubt and shame over what you endured in your relationship, it is crucial to be kind to yourself when you begin to reflect on the connection. Dealing through emotions of embarrassment, humiliation, or guilt over how horrible the relationship was is nearly always the initial step in recovery.

Fourthly, the purpose of emotional healing is emotional suffering. The emotional issue which has been ignored is afterward faced as a result. Relief is felt at this point because avoiding issues might make them worse. To overcome the emotional blockade, be prepared. Do be honest with yourself when analyzing emotional issues. After recognizing the emotional causes, confront them.

Try to acknowledge your unpleasant emotions after you've faced them, and you should start to feel better.

Finally, many of you have likely "settled" into relationships with toxic or violent dynamics, and this may have something to do with your perceptions of your self-worth and level of confidence. It may be difficult to believe that anyone will appreciate being in a relationship with you if there have been times when your character has been undermined. As just a result, you can attract those who don't value you.

It can be challenging to heal. And I won't lie, that's scary. This healing was not something I would say you entered with the intention of having fun. You might feel hesitant and resist entering, which can make you anxious.

There may always be memories, emotions, ideas, feelings, tears, and laughter associated with former people you have spent your life with; that emptiness would eventually heal and replace with joy. The search for real love is part of the human experience. The most crucial action in a relationship and also the most crucial action after ending one is learning to love oneself. Always "check in" to ensure you are mentally and emotionally recovering from your prior trauma. Keep being loyal to who you are. Give yourself the time and space to mourn as much as you need to. Understanding to appreciate yourself more than you did even before the relationship is crucial to learning how to do so. Consider the process of healing an opportunity to better understand oneself and develop self-compassion.

CHAPTER 16
HEALING FROM EMOTIONAL TRAUMA

Romantic connections may come and go throughout our lives. Unfortunately, breaking up with someone always results in heartache. Even if this is entirely natural, there might be more remaining below the surface. After a relationship has ended, it's normal to feel insecure. It's normal to need some time to recover after a relationship ends; wearing sweats and binge-watching your favorite movies are all part of the recovery process. However, overcoming relationship trauma is very different from going through the post-breakup blues.

It might be difficult to leave a toxic or abusive relationship behind. The trauma of being in a toxic relationship can either have short-term or long-term repercussions on your emotional health. Relationship trauma results whenever physical, mental, or sexual abuse occurs in an emotional relationship.
Traumatic relationships could have an impact on a person's daily life.

Sometimes if they like someone, many trauma survivors have a hard time believing them and have trouble developing romantic relationships. It's difficult to let go of the previous, particularly when trying to move on after a toxic relationship.

What Is Emotional Trauma?

Some emotions are triggered by our recollections. Some recollections are good, while others could be bad. They either make us feel good or awful when we think of them. They could make us laugh or cry depending on how much attention we give them. Without our conscious attention, some memories, though, have a more significant impact on us.

Emotional trauma might well be brought on by painful memories that are difficult to let go of. We occasionally encounter what seems like irreversible effects from unpleasant events, unpleasant feelings, or the intense pain of an unforgettable moment. Trauma then enters the picture. An extremely upsetting or unsettling encounter is referred to as trauma. The traumatic events in our lives cannot be changed, and they may still have an impact on us in the future.

Extremely stressful circumstances that shatter your feeling of security and leave you feeling vulnerable in a stressful environment might lead to emotional trauma. You may struggle with troubling feelings, memories, and anxiety as a result of trauma. You might also experience feelings of numbness, alienation, and lack of confidence in other people.

Traumatic events frequently involve a danger to one's life or physical safety. However, they can also be caused by any circumstance that makes you feel helpless and alone. Your emotional reaction to the incident, not the objective facts, determines whether it qualifies as traumatic. You're more inclined to make poor decisions when you feel fearful and helpless.

How to Heal From Emotional Trauma

It varies from person to person how they recover from psychological and emotional trauma. Recognizing what you're in for is the first step in recovering from your relationship trauma. It is quite simple to relapse into the abuse cycle if you are not prepared to accept your situation and move on. as soon as you have safely left your toxic relationship and are prepared to end the pattern. A person's methods may not be effective for another. The solutions listed below may aid in your quest for healing, but not everyone will travel the same route. Professional counseling from a behavioral health specialist could be helpful if you feel hopeless or overtaken by an experience.

- **The secret is patience:** You must be ready to be patient with your partner if you have chosen to continue in a relationship despite all the negative repercussions of the trauma. You might not first feel optimistic about the healing process, but then as you observe your partner making adjustments, you will gradually start to feel better.

- **Exercise and movement:** This might help you to improve the nervous system's recovery as trauma disturbs your body's natural balance. A half-hour or longer workout helps with both physical and psychological well-being. It also doesn't have to happen all at once. It is just as beneficial to fit in a few ten-minute workout sessions throughout the day. The finest exercises are rhythmic ones that use both arms and legs. While engaging in physical activities like yoga, kung fu, weightlifting, rock climbing, or boxing, include awareness by paying close attention to your movements. This is a fantastic approach to shifting your focus from unfavorable ideas. Pay attention to how your body reacts as you move, the pattern of your breath, the feel of the earth beneath your feet, or the sensation of the breeze on your skin. While performing useful tasks, being fully conscious of these sensations puts you in the present and gives you a deeper sense of fulfillment. This promotes mindfulness, tranquility, and calm.

- **Connect with others:** Accept that lunch invite or sign up for a hobby club to give you fresh and different things to think about because connecting with others is an important component of healing. A little "me-time" is fine, but too much could be unhealthy. Consider contacting a behavioral health professional for assistance if talking to your friends or family causes you any discomfort. You can express your emotions here without fear of criticism.

  Counselors may offer insight into your ideas as well as suggestions for improving your outlook. Take part in social events. To keep your mind off unpleasant memories and situations, try to engage in "regular" activities. Find new friends or rekindle old friendships and important prior relationships. Being around people can improve your mood. Consider attending a class or participating in activities to meet people who have similar interests to your own.

- **Live in the present:** It is essential that you put your attention on the present and your future as you work on mending rather than dwelling on the past. Positive thinking would become the pattern as you create new constructive habits with your companion. It is crucial to concentrate on the positive changes happening right now because if you are still hooked on the past, you could easily relapse into destructive patterns.

- **Taking better care of yourself:** Activities that lower stress and advance emotional and physical well-being are considered self-care. These pursuits are nourishing, satisfying, and beneficial. Great self reduces stress, fosters self-love, and teaches you to depend on yourself for happiness rather than a controlling partner. Several examples of self-care include:
    - Journaling
    - Taking in music
    - Yoga, meditation, and Tai Chi are examples of relaxation techniques.
    - Having a restful night's sleep
    - Eating healthy
    - Spending time with loved ones you can trust

- **Create healthy relationships:** Give yourself permission to interact with others who are both physically and emotionally secure. Exercise effective communication and self-advocacy. Your capacity to create healthy attachments is strengthened by engaging in good interactions.

- **Call for Support:** You may feel better if you really can find solace with a behavioral health professional, spiritual guide, or dependable family member. It might not be necessary to go into depth about your tragedy, but we could all use a sympathetic ear that won't pass judgment. Become a part of a support network for trauma victims. Making connections with people who can relate with you because they have also been through similar experiences could motivate you, make you feel less alone, and speed up your healing.

- **Volunteer:** It's a terrific approach to regaining your sense of power to help others. You'll feel more fulfilled, less helpless, and reminded of your abilities when you realize that you're somehow improving the lives of other people.

- **Therapy helps:** Being open and honest with your family and friends after leaving an abusive relationship might occasionally be challenging. Again, you might have thoughts of guilt and uncertainty. It may be time to get professional assistance if this is the situation with you. Eye movement desensitization and reprocessing, sometimes known as EMDR, is a method of treatment that can be applied. Talking about your circumstances is difficult or maybe impossible due to the physical reactions associated with trauma. You may learn and recover together by utilizing EMDR plus emotional transformation therapy (ETT).

If you are still suffering from the repercussions of a traumatic relationship, know that you can always recover. If you are devoted to adopting new approaches to thinking and addressing your relationships, it is possible to have meaningful relationships after trauma. Individuals who have gone through trauma find it difficult to reach out in times of need or ask for assistance. Receiving a compliment, for example, may be difficult despite its seeming simplicity.

But to lead a full and balanced life, one must be able to overcome these doubts and hesitations. If you put the techniques covered in this chapter into practice, you'll be well on your journey to recovering from the wounds. A counselor or psychologist with therapeutic experience could assist you in making progress if you are having trouble recovering on your own.

CHAPTER 17
HOW TO CREATE HEALTHY RELATIONSHIPS

Having been in a relationship with a toxic partner helped you understand what things you do not want in a relationship. You need to be wise while choosing your next partner and actively work towards the relationship to ensure it is a healthy relationship. A healthy relationship will help you grow as an individual and allow you to be yourself, both in the relationship and outside the relationship. Everyone shares a different bond with their partners, but here is a list of a few things that everyone can follow to create a happy and healthy relationship.

DO NOT FEAR AWAY FROM DISAGREEMENTS

It is a tendency in most individuals to suppress their needs in front of their partner after coming out of an unhealthy relationship. It is almost as if you are afraid of disagreements as they may cause conflict between the two, and you are afraid of that. By doing this, you are bottling up emotions within yourself, and you are now being responsible for creating toxicity in the relationship. Just like you would like complete transparency from your partner, your partner deserves the same. To create a healthy relationship, you must not fear away from respectful disagreements. Tell them what is bothering you, and they will listen to you. The foundation of a healthy relationship lies in being able to maintain your individualities in and out of the relationship. You need to discuss this with your partner; both parties need to express their feelings, and the other needs to be able to actively listen to it without any judgment or ill intentions. If you can resolve differences by communicating well, then that is a major step toward creating a healthy relationship.

BE AN ACTIVE LISTENER IN THE RELATIONSHIP

You have heard it numerous times - be a good speaker or a communicator but what is not talked about enough is that you need to be a good listener as well to maintain a healthy relationship. Communication is the key to a healthy relationship, and communication involves active listening as well. When you are talking or your partner is talking, the other person needs to listen. Hearing is one thing, and listening is different. Listen to your partner carefully, and you will observe minute details. Couples in a healthy relationship are always listening to each other, they may or may not agree with each other, but they respect each other's opinions.

The minute you start actively listening to your partner, you will observe intonations in your partner's voice, even if they are subtle. It will help you understand how they truly feel about something or a situation. There is nothing more beautiful than your romantic partner listening to you and understanding you. Another major reason why you must practice active listening is that it will help you resolve conflicts much more easily. When you do not know what is bothering you, how can you work towards resolving it? When your partner expresses their point of annoyance to you, you should not get defensive but rather listen to them. It will not cause you to accept or agree to what they are saying but will help you both find common ground and resolve matters faster.

CREATE AND MAINTAIN HEALTHY BOUNDARIES

Creating and maintaining boundaries is equally important to create and maintain a healthy relationship. Boundaries are not set just to maintain distance from each other but to ensure you are giving enough space to each other to pursue things that you love doing as an individual. A relationship becomes toxic when one partner starts being the dominating one, dominating their partner to do things they like and the way they like. This takes away the individuality of the subservient partner. If you faced this in your toxic relationship, then you must know it makes you feel suffocated and lost. Thus this has to be avoided, and the best way to do so is by giving each other ample space through maintaining healthy boundaries.

Let us say you want to spend all your free time with your partner, but they want to spend limited time with you. In such circumstances, you both need to find common ground and set a boundary on how much time you both need to spend together. This is just an example; you should also set boundaries to meet with your friends, get your work done, and be able to spend some alone time that will help you introspect your relationship better. I have already discussed the various methods through which you can set boundaries in Chapter 11.

TREAT YOUR PARTNER THE WAY YOU WANT TO BE TREATED

The best way to create and maintain a healthy relationship is by treating your partner the way you want to be treated. Do you want your problems to be resolved on the same day by talking? Then show it to your partner. Initiate a conversation, and be the first to say sorry if you have done something wrong. This will encourage your partner to do the same. Similarly, be affectionate to your partner, shower them with all your love and gifts occasionally, and treat them with respect. Similarly, observe the way they treat you and pick up their traits as well. Do not wait for them to make a move, go ahead and treat them the way you want to be treated. If required, you can also express to them your needs and requirements.

DO NOT HIDE YOUR TRUE SELF FROM YOUR PARTNER

A healthy relationship is created when the two people in it are real. You may have had a bad experience, but that does not mean you will need to wear a mask throughout your life. When you are in a relationship with the right person, you will not need to hide your true self. Be vulnerable and open your heart to them. Tell them about your likes and dislikes, even about your experience. Being completely honest with yourself and your partner will ensure your relationship is healthy. Do not forget to tell your partner what you need from the relationship or what is bothering you. It is toxic behavior when you or your partner expect the other to guess things. A major benefit of staying authentic in a relationship is you will have more fun as you will not have the stress of maintaining a false image of yourself at all times.

CONNECT EMOTIONALLY

A healthy relationship is more than just co-existing; it is about understanding each other and connecting on an emotional level. You need to fulfill each other emotionally as well and make each other feel loved. If you see your partner feeling low, ask them what is bothering them and give emotional support if they need it or a warm hug if they want to be just heard. Make your relationship a safe space for both of you to be vulnerable. You both need to be able to share your deepest and darkest fears and emotions without getting judged. If you can achieve that in your relationship, then there is no doubt that you are meant for each other.

PRACTICE SELF LOVE AND ENCOURAGE YOUR PARTNER TO DO THE SAME

No love can ever be enough for you if you do not love yourself. Thus, even before getting into a relationship, you need to start practicing self-love and self-care. Of course, the purpose of a relationship is to be loved and feel loved, but it is not the responsibility of your partner to fill the void that you have created by not loving yourself. You need to be able to love yourself equally as much as you love your partner; only then will you feel satisfied in a relationship. Otherwise, no matter how much your partner loves you, you will still want more, and it is not healthy for either of you. Thus, do not forget to shower love on yourself even while in a relationship and encourage your partner to do the same.

BALANCE ALL YOUR RELATIONSHIPS

Being in a relationship does not mean you need to cut down on relationships with all your friends and family. You must be able to balance all your relationships and encourage your partner to do the same. A relationship is healthy when both partners support each other's relationships outside their relationship.

Do not be afraid to open your heart again; not everyone is the same. If life has given you a chance, you need to take full advantage of it. In the next chapter, I will discuss a few important points that will help you become a better version of yourself post a toxic relationship.

CHAPTER 18
TIPS TO KEEP IN MIND

Toxic relationships impact different people differently, but what remains common is the pain and difficulty moving on from it. Some individuals find it difficult to forget their partners even after knowing they have been toxic and harmful to them. You may have followed all the steps mentioned in the book, yet there can come times when you find yourself back to level 0. This is a temporary state, and with a little push, you can go back to being a confident person again. In this chapter, I will share a few tips that will help you stay positive in life after having moved on from your toxic relationship. These tips will also help you to attract healthy love instead of toxic people.

KEEP CONNECTION WITH EMOTIONALLY HEALTHY INDIVIDUALS

In most toxic relationships, the submissive partner loses touch with all their trusted family members and friends. This happens as a toxic partner sees your emotionally healthy and trusted friends as a threat to themselves and the relationship and ensures you are completely cut off from them. After moving on from a toxic relationship, you are free to connect with all your friends and family members. However, there might be a problem from your side - you feel trepidation to go back and reconnect with them. This happens out of guilt or fear of being judged or rejected. Remember, they are your well-wishers, and they will understand where you are coming from. Trust me when I say this, they will be proud of you for saving yourself from the destructive relationship. Talk to your friends, as sometimes a simple conversation helps to get things back to being normal.

If you still need time, do not discuss your relationship instantly with them; instead, start a conversation by saying simple things like: "I have been distant lately, but I would like to connect back with you." In most cases, you will regain your trusted friends back in your life again, but you need to be slightly cautious.
You need to be observant as some dynamics might have changed while you were away, and some friends may seem a little indifferent towards you.

You have just gotten off of a battle and do not need to get into another one. Thus keep connection with only those friends who are emotionally healthy and wait till you completely heal to connect back with the difficult people in your life.

DO NOT BE AFRAID TO SHARE YOUR JOURNEY

It is not your fault that you got stuck in a toxic relationship; you had simply fallen in love with the wrong person or maybe at the wrong time. There is nothing wrong with you to make you feel ashamed to tell your side of the story to the world.
If you are not ready, take your time. Write your entire experience in a journal; that way, you can both vent out and process the entire experience. Whatever you do, share your experience instead of bottling it up within yourself and regretting it.

BE KIND AND TRUTHFUL TO YOURSELF

I will repeat this as many times as possible, as you need to be kind to yourself. No matter what, do not blame yourself for everything. You may tend to tow back in time and look at the faults that landed you in certain situations and talk extremely harshly with yourself. This is the worst thing that you can do to yourself. Imagine your loved one has been in a toxic relationship and has just moved on. Would you talk to them in the same tone as you are talking to yourself? No, right? Then why should you treat yourself badly?

Be kind to yourself and stop lying to yourself that it is because of you that you ended up being in a mess. A toxic partner has too much power over you and the way they manipulate you that it is not possible for you to identify the toxicity without proper guidance until some visible damage has been made. Even if you did let go of certain behaviors after sensing something, stop blaming yourself for that. You were in love and had all the good intentions and naturally expected the same thing in return. Accept this fact and always be kind to yourself else you may end up self-sabotaging yourself and your future.

DO NOT STAY STUCK IN THE PAST

The process of recovery can be turbulent, and you may often be tempted to look back on the past, take notes and plan for the future. Is there any guarantee that things will move in the same way as they used to before? Looking back at the past time and again is only going to trap you in the past. You have moved on from the relationship, the suffering, and all the mental trauma, then why do you want to go back in time again? As discussed in the previous point, when you are re-visiting the past, you are forcefully finding your faults and blaming and being unkind to yourself. So you have to stop it and love in the present.

TRY TO INVOLVE YOURSELF IN VOLUNTARY SERVICES

As per several studies, involving yourself in voluntary services decreases the symptoms of depression and anxiety. Moreover, it is a way to connect back with community people and work together towards something meaningful. This may help you gain back your lost self-esteem and help you find a purpose in life.

Involving yourself in voluntary services for the unfortunate ones will help you realize that life is so beautiful and worth living to the fullest. It will instill a sense of gratefulness in you and help you forget about the past gradually and allow you to look forward. If you involve yourself in social services for animals, it will bring you joy. Surrounding yourself with innocent animals will only fill your life with gratitude and a sense of joy. More than anything, you will identify there is so much more to life than one failed relationship.

Make sure you are looking at the purpose of the organization thoroughly before signing up for the voluntary services. Some voluntary services can be extreme for you, and you need to weigh that before joining in. Also, it will only be more advantageous if you join an organization that supports the well-being of voluntary workers.

DO NOT BE AFRAID TO OPEN YOUR HEART AGAIN

Were you madly in love with your ex? You thought they were the one for you? You had plans to marry him or her? Yet they did what they did, and now you feel you are not meant for love.

My dear reader, this is the extreme low that you may get to, and it is not unnatural. Others feel or have felt the same way. You have to accept that your partner was not the right one for you, and because of them, you can not close your heart. Treat your toxic relationship as yet another tough life lesson, and open your heart for love again. I am not asking you to do it right away; take your time to heal your heart and yourself but do not be afraid of love.

TAKE HELP FROM PROFESSIONALS

When you have been in a toxic relationship for years, then it can get extremely difficult to move on. People often tend to pick up unhealthy habits. If you are feeling extremely low and nothing seems to help, talk to a professional. After a toxic relationship where you have been constantly abused or exploited, it is only normal to feel symptoms of post-traumatic stress disorder. You may have difficulty trusting anyone or have difficulty going about with your everyday life. In that situation, please consider getting help from a professional, as it helps a great deal. Different people heal differently; some are quick to move on, while others may need that extra help, and there is nothing wrong with either. Please talk to a professional, as the most important thing to achieve post a toxic breakup is to get yourself back and lead a healthy life.

I must mention how proud I am of you that you have made it this far in the book. You are already a warrior if you have managed to break free from the unhealthy cage of the toxic relationship. Remember, in life, you have good days and bad days, and right now, you are in the transition phase. Soon there will be better and brighter days; just hang in there a little longer, soldier, and keep striding forward.

CONCLUSION

You have reached the end of *Healing From Toxic Relationships: When to Walk Away*. How to Leave Behind the Past. Let's hope it was full of useful information and was able to deliver the tools you require to attain your goals, no matter what they are.

All you need to do now is to use all the information from this guidebook to take back charge of your life. Toxic relationships can destroy your life. It is necessary to be aware of the toxic traits before things go out of hand. The tips and suggestions that you came across in this book can surely help you get out of toxic relationships.

Always remember that getting out of toxic relationships is not that easy. Toxic people might cage you with tactics that might seem impossible to break. Try to be patient and turn on your defensive shield whenever you sense any kind of toxicity. Negative people will be around you all the time. All that matters is the way you deal with them for a better life.

Don't go! Just one last thing!
If you liked this book or found it useful, I'd appreciate it if you could leave a quick review on Amazon. Your support is greatly appreciated, and I personally read all of the reviews in order to obtain feedbacks and improve the book.

Thanks for your help and support!

Hey! Don't miss my other books! They for sure can add more value to your knowledge! Here are the following:

. **Effective Communication in Relationships**: How to Create a Loving and Healthy Relationship Through the Power of Coherence, Listening, and Empathy

Because communication is so integral to your entire relationship and is even one of the three key pillars in a healthy relationship, not being able to communicate effectively is a sure way to condemn your relationship to failure. However, communication is something you can develop through diligence and effort. You can train yourself to become better at communicating. Much like practice will make you stronger, you can use repeated practice at various communication-building exercises to become better at communicating effectively with your partner, and this book intends to teach you several skills you can use exactly for that process.

. **Effective Communication in the Workplace**: How As a Woman - Improve Your Interpersonal Communication with Assertiveness and Cogency in Your Workplace

Do you struggle in the workplace? No matter how hard you may try to be an effective employee, do you find that you somehow always manage to make things worse? You may try to convey that one thing is needed, but instead, there is nothing but chaos when everyone tries to do the exact opposite due to your own failure to communicate clearly and effectively. Maybe you attempt to say one thing but it is misconstrued as something else. Perhaps you simply cannot manage to discuss your own thoughts and feelings without shutting down because you are too self-conscious or shy, so when you do try or you do feel put on the spot, you freeze. Through reading this book, you will develop the skill set necessary to be effective at communicating in professional settings

. **How Highly Effective People Speak**: How to High Perform in Speaking in Order to Influence Everyone in Any Situation

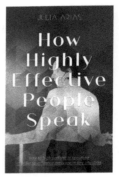

Discover the Secrets To Becoming a Highly Effective Speaker and Become a Master of Public Speaking!
Have you ever stood in front of a crowd and panicked because you didn't know what to do?
Have you ever been a speaker in an event and the people in the audience were looking at their phones or talking among themselves?
Are you looking for a way to improve your public speaking skills and be able to influence big crowds?
If your answer is **YES***, this book is for you!*

It's difficult to be an effective speaker when you're not used to speaking in front of a crowd. It's even more difficult to influence a crowd when you have raging anxiety inside of you.
Being able to influence an audience sounds like a difficult task. Without the proper training and the right guide, it's impossible to take control of the audience's attention.

Luckily for you, this guidebook on How Highly Effective People Speak is a true game-changer! This book will teach you all the essentials towards becoming a highly effective speaker and will help you enhance your powers of persuasion even in big crowds!

. Insecure in Love: How To Increase Your Value And Your Self-Esteem

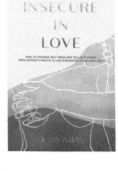

The root of your problems and the place that the anxiety, uncertainty, and insecurity stem from is self-doubt. All of that leads to discomfort, and feeling uncomfortable in your relationship can be very painful and disturbing. You might constantly feel as if your partner is going to break up with you. As a result, you might have a hard time trusting them not to betray you.

Alternatively, you may believe that the bond has been deteriorating for some time and that the pillars are starting to crumble. However, there is no need for any concern; there is a way to change all of that, and this book will show you how to do it the simplest way possible.

Milton Keynes UK
Ingram Content Group UK Ltd.
UKHW032048201124
451474UK00005B/364